Rev. A. Schabow
Pastor Schabow

SAINT PAUL

A Brief Series of Evening Texts Made
Ready for Pulpit Work

BY

R. C. H. LENSKI

"By the grace of God I am what I am."—*1 Cor. 15, 10.*

1916
LUTHERAN BOOK CONCERN
Columbus, Ohio

A WORD OF INTRODUCTION.

THE preparation of the Sunday morning sermon usually takes the greater part of a preacher's available time and the best part of his strength; the Sunday evening sermon then receives what may be left. This handicap for the latter is increased by the fact, that we have a fine variety of text selections ready to hand for the Sunday morning sermons, and this for the entire church year, while there is nothing at all of the same character for the Sunday evening sermon. The preacher is compelled to make his own selections from the Scriptures as he may see fit, either step by step from one Sunday evening to the next, or in short lines of texts for a number of consecutive Sunday evenings. In either case, however, he finds few helps at hand to lighten, direct, and expedite his work of sermon preparation; he does the best he can — and sometimes not quite the best, — and when he feels that the result falls short of what he desires, he is not pleased. This is the situation which has prompted the author to undertake the preparation of a small volume of text studies on St. Paul. It is his intention, if the work meets with approval, and time and health permit, to continue with other similar volumes containing about eight to twelve texts, each set constituting a distinct series by itself. One might be on St. Peter, another on St. John, a third on the Congregation and Congregational Life, a fourth on "What the Spirit Saith Unto the Churches," *etc., etc.*

A Word of Introduction.

This program might be modified, and also extended, as the brethren desire. The sole object in this first effort is to furnish abundant sound and workable material for that part of the preacher's task which needs it almost more than any other, and in doing this to stimulate those who use this material to increase their own efforts, and thus the more surely to obtain greater and better results.

The texts here offered all pertain directly to St. Paul. Those from his writings are connected as fully as possible with his own person, faith, work, and character. On some of these texts more than one sermon may be preached, thus lengthening the series as may be desired. The hints and outlines are added for their suggestive value, to further stimulate the thought and planning of the preacher when he has worked into the substance of the text and begins to formulate his material for the sermon proper. Several of the texts here offered belong to the richest and most precious portions of Scripture; all nine, it is hoped, will be found serviceable for the object in view.

May God's blessing attend this effort to serve his holy church.

THE AUTHOR.

February 14, 1916.

CONTENTS.

	PAGE
THE PHARISEE, Acts 7, 58-8, 4	9
THE CHRISTIAN, Acts 9, 1-9 and 17-22	39
THE MISSIONARY, Acts 14, 1-7	68
THE PREACHER OF JUSTIFICATION, Rom. 3, 20-26	90
THE MAN OF LOVE, 1 Cor. 13, 1-13	122
A MINISTER OF MINISTERS, 1 Tim. 3, 1-7	154
THE APOSTLE OF HOPE, 1 Cor. 15, 42b-49	183
IN CHAINS, Acts 26, 22-30	206
FACING THE END, 2 Tim. 4, 16-18	230

SAINT PAUL

THE PHARISEE.
Acts 7, 58 — 8, 4.

Whoever sets out to preach on what the Holy Scriptures record concerning the Apostle St. Paul must give special heed to three things: first, the wonder of divine grace wrought in this man's own person, when from a passionate, bloodthirsty Pharisee he was changed into a fervent believer and apostle of Jesus Christ; secondly, the wonders of divine grace wrought through this man's tireless zeal and devotion, when he evangelized Asia Minor and parts of southern Europe; and finally, the wonders of divine grace and truth, which the Holy Ghost by this man's inspired pen set down for the illumination of all future ages. First a Pharisee; then a Christian; then a missionary; then an inspired writer; finally a martyr for the faith; surely a theme worthy of the greatest masters our pulpits will ever see.

In any review of what God wrought in and through this man, especially in a survey intended for the pulpits of our day, we must understand well the kind of man God here first dealt with. It is one whom we all, if we met him in life to-day, would in our human judgment pronounce hopeless as far as bringing him to Christ is concerned. The Scriptures purposely introduce him to us for the first time when the blood of the first martyr stained the stones that were used in his murder. St. Luke might have mentioned Saul at an earlier point in his narrative, namely when he records Stephen's victorious disputes with the Jews in the synagogues of the Libertines, the Cyrenians, the Alexandrians, and them of Cilicia and Asia, in Jerusalem. We must recall that Tarsus, the home of Saul, was a city of Cilicia. The entire account of St. Luke justifies the conclusion that Saul was implicated in these disputes with Stephen, but he is not mentioned by name until the tragedy of this first martyr comes to its climax. But now that his name is brought forward, at once all the dark colors are put into the portrait. It is he who fans the blaze of Jewish bigotry and hate into the first "great persecution" (διωγμὸς μέγας) of the followers of Jesus, and who makes himself the chief agent of this terrible and in part bloody work. He afterwards described himself at this period of his life as "a blasphemer, and a persecutor, and injurious," 1 Tim. 1, 13. He laid waste the church; he spared neither men nor women; he haled them to prison; punished them oftentimes in all the synagogues; strove to make them blaspheme the name of Jesus; and when they were put to death because of their steadfastness, it was his vote that invariably went against them, though others might hesitate. Acts 26, 10-11. Could a darker picture be drawn? Could a more hopeless case, humanly speaking, be conceived? And yet divine grace triumphed: it was this man who by the grace of God in Christ Jesus came to be one of the foremost, if not *the* foremost of the apostles of the Lord. He who helped bring Stephen and others to a bloody death because of their faith in Christ and his Word, became the instrument to bring thousands to life everlasting through faith in this Christ and his saving Word.

These, then, are some of the lines we must draw in treating the first text here presented on St. Paul: Saul — the Pharisee — the most violent hater of Christ and his followers — the most bitter opponent of the Gospel and its doctrine of salvation by grace without works, — yet Christ's grace made him a chosen instrument for his work among men. It is altogether a picture so dramatic in its essentials, as well as in its setting, that it leaves far behind anything ever portrayed by mere genius in secular literature. Let the gripping interest of it enter the preacher's heart when he proceeds to set God's work in this man's heart and life before his hearers. This captive of the Gospel shows all its triumphant power in fullest, grandest measure. And wielding such a Gospel among men to-day, there is only one thing for us to do, namely to go forth with triumphant assurance and joy in our hearts, against any and all the bulwarks that Satan may erect. He who stormed this citadel is bound to win again and again.

The story of Stephen is the background for what we desire to gather from our text concerning the Pharisee Saul. Chosen as one of the seven deacons, to minister unto the poor, in order to release the apostles from the duty of serving tables (Acts 6, 1, *etc.*), Stephen proved to be "a man full of faith and of the Holy Ghost;" for besides the special duties allotted to him and his companions in this diaconate he used the talents and spiritual gifts bestowed upon him by God to carry the Gospel forward in the different synagogues of Jerusalem. He chose the synagogues of the so-called Hellenists or Grecian Jews, and came into sharp conflict with two of these, namely the synagogue of the Libertines, and of the Cyrenians, and of the Alexandrians, and the synagogue of them of Cilicia and of Asia (Luke, in Acts 6, 9, marks the division into two: τινες τῶν ἐκ . . . καὶ τῶν ἀπὸ . . .). Some of these Grecian Jews had already come to faith, for they were the ones who complained about the neglect of their widows in the daily ministrations, Acts 6, 1. These were the Jews whose every-day language was Greek, who accordingly used the Septuagint translation as their Bible, who were open to many of the ideas of Greek culture and philosophy (for instance Philo), and whose great center of influence was Alexandria in Egypt. While scattered extensively through the countries where Greek was the medium of intercourse, we see that they were numerous and powerful in Jerusalem itself. We dare not be hasty in drawing the conclusion that Stephen originally belonged to this class, for we see that in one of their synagogues he came in contact with Saul, who cannot be classed as a Hellenist, for he calls himself a "Hebrew of the Hebrews." This refers to the other great class of Jews, called "the Hebrews," Acts 6, 1; these were Aramæan Jews, whose language in daily life was the Aramaic, who used the Targums or Chaldee paraphrases in working with the Scriptures, whose homes were mostly in Palestine, Syria, and the countries of the Tigris. But while Saul came from this great class of Jews, and in his home training, under his Pharisee father, and under the teaching of Rabbi Gamaliel at Jerusalem, imbibed the sterner spirit of the Hebrews, he had broadened out beyond the things they stood for. We see that he knew Greek from his boyhood days on, that he was acquainted with the Greek literature of the day, that he was fully conversant with the Septuagint, and that he did not hold himself aloof from the Hellenistic Jews. His native town was Tarsus in Cilicia, and it is thus that we find him in the synagogue of the Cilicians in Jerusalem, when there the conflict with Stephen waxed hot, and when none of those zealots for the old faith and traditions were able to withstand the wisdom and the Spirit by which Stephen spoke, Acts 6, 10.

We know what happened: foul means were employed when fair means failed; perjurers were hired (6, 11); the people and the Sanhedrim were stirred up; Stephen was brought to trial; he made a defense which at the same time laid bare the chief sin of Israel in all ages and especially in this last age. Stephen spoke at length on God's gracious dealings which Israel constantly rewarded with unbelieving disobedience. 1) He was so far from blaspheming God that he acknowledged him in the fullest possible way by the manner in which he recounted the story of the patriarchs, Israel's progenitors; but he wove in the bitter story of Joseph, whose brothers' jealousy sold him into Egypt. 2) He likewise refuted the charge of blaspheming Moses and the Law, by acknowledging both in a signal manner; but he showed that Israel opposed Moses who testified of Christ, made the golden calf, and went so far in its idolatry in the wilderness that God abandoned the whole nation "to serve the host of heaven" (sun, moon, and stars). 3) Nor had he blasphemed the temple, for he acknowledged both the tabernacle and the Solomonic temple, though God is infinitely greater than both. Now, however, with the picture complete, Stephen turned upon his accusers and judges, and, like one of the old time prophets, hurled the full accusations of the Law against them: they had completed the work of their wicked forefathers who had killed the prophets, by themselves becoming the betrayers and murderers of the Righteous One of whom the prophets had testified. This precipitated the tragedy. Stephen, no doubt, meant to follow the blows of the Law by a strong Gospel appeal. Instead, the Savior himself intervenes by revealing himself in his glory at the right hand of God, causing Stephen to exclaim: "Behold, I see the heavens opened, and the Son of man standing at the right hand of God." As Saul afterwards, when on the road to Damascus, so the Jews here knew with whom they had to do: the Son of man in glory. But their unbelief would not only not yield, it drove them on to commit another bloody outrage, to shed the blood of the first martyr of our holy Christian religion.

And Saul was there. Let us remember that.

(57) **But they cried out with a loud voice, and stopped their ears, and rushed upon him with one accord;** (58) **and they cast him out of the city, and stoned him.**

The word κράζω here is equal to our English scream or yell. We have the participle in Greek, followed by a finite verb, where in English the two actions are simply coordinated: "they cried out and stopped their ears." The aorist participle is at times simultaneous with the following aorist tense of the main verb; so here, the screams and yells of the outraged crowd were uttered while they held their ears shut. The singular φωνῇ μεγάλῃ, "with a voice that was loud," gives in one term the effect of what the many did at the same moment: the noise was one great outburst of sound. — **And stopped their ears,** συνέσχον, like the following ὥρμησαν, has the historical aorist which simply records the fact as such. To stop the ears and to yell at top voice meant, of course, in a double way to prevent any further utterance of Stephen from reaching them. It was the strongest kind of a verdict that not only in the past had he spoken, but was now continuing to speak, and in the most intolerable way, damnable blasphemy. Meyer's idea that the Sanhedrists began this yelling and stopping the ears, and especially that they made the first move in rushing upon Stephen, is entirely in keeping with the situation as described by Luke. The Sanhedrists, we may say, would be affected the more by Stephen's last utterance, because this vividly reminded them of the ominous prophecy of Jesus: "Hereafter shall ye see the Son of man sitting on the right hand of power, and coming in the clouds of heaven." Matth. 26, 64. At that time, too, they had given the verdict: "He hath spoken blasphemy . . . He is guilty of death." But here the added sting of the reference to Jesus at God's right hand in glory and power stirs them to immediate violence against Stephen. They will not hear it said or even hinted that Jesus shall make his word to them true. — **And rushed upon him with one accord,** both to stop him from saying anything further, and also to drag him away to immediate death. The dreadful unanimity of all present is shown by the addition of ὁμοθυμαδόν. There was no one to advise even a moment's delay or second and soberer thought. This blaze of sudden fury was characteristic of the Jews on many similar occasions. Here, in the beginning, the regular forms of trial were used with Stephen: after the formal charge was preferred, and substantiated by the testimony of the witnesses brought forward, the high priest, as the presiding judge, demanded of the accused: "Are these things so?" (Acts 7, 1), and then the defendant was permitted to make answer to the charge. But when he was through, all forms of legal and regular procedure were for the moment cast to the winds. The utterance of what they deemed the worst kind of blasphemy, right in the presence of the High Court itself, carried them away and overthrew the formalities they had held to up to this point.

(58) **And they cast him out of the city** *etc.* The action of ἐκβαλόντες precedes that of ἐλιθοβόλουν. On another occasion the Jews took up stones against Jesus in Solomon's porch, to stone him for blasphemy then and there, John 10, 31. Also when Jesus warned the Jews of the bloodguilt they were heaping upon themselves, he mentioned the blood of Zacharias, son of Barachias, whom they had slain between the temple building and the altar in front of it, Matth. 23, 35. In the case of blasphemy the Jews had an explicit command: "He that blasphemeth the name of the Lord, he shall surely be put to death, and all the congregation shall certainly stone him," Lev. 24, 16. This law was given in connection with an actual case of blasphemy, in regard to which the divine direction had been sought, and which for this blasphemer included that he be brought forth without the camp and there stoned (verse 14). While such bringing forth was not made a general command, we still see pecu-

liar instances in which it was observed. Innocent Naboth was "carried forth out of the city and stoned with stones, that he died," 1 Kgs. 21, 13; and the charge against him was blasphemy. The people of Nazareth led Jesus forth, when they wanted to make away with him, Luke 4, 29. And afterwards Jesus did actually "suffer without the gate," Heb. 13, 12. Summary procedures in the lawless application of the law, or in lawlessly satisfying the supposed claims of justice, seem after all to demand a certain line of formality, with all their undue haste, possibly in order to satisfy the feeling that otherwise the act might look too much like a mere crime of violence. So Stephen was not dragged out into the street and stoned close to the hall of trial; he was taken out of the city entirely, in this respect making his death like that of his Lord and Savior before him. It is a strange trait of perverted human nature thus to cling to some empty outward formality, and to observe it perhaps at great expense and trouble, while the deep essentials of the law, justice, right, godliness, and holiness are utterly gone.—**And stoned him,** ἐλιθοβόλουν, imperf. tense: they were stoning, or continued to stone him; this, following the previous aorists, dwells as it were upon the sad and terrible fact, pictures it and describes it to the mind. The dragging out, too, took some time, but though also violent and dreadful, it is the stoning that Luke by this tense lays the emphasis on. No need here to have the aorist in order to show that the bloody deed was completed and this martyr stoned to death; Luke means to tell us that in a more impressive way. Yes, Stephen at last lay lifeless under the heavy rock that was used to crush his loins and his chest. We may well question just how the stoning was done here. The old way was to throw the condemned man down and to crush his loins with a great rock, then if necessary his breast; if not dead then many stones were hurled upon him. This way may have been used here; or the general stoning, after the witnesses had cast the first stones, may have set in at once. Whatever the Jews might say of it, they here contravened the law of their rulers, the Romans, who alone could inflict capital punishment. But it need not surprise us to find that the thing was done with impunity, at least in this case. Pilate had consented to Jesus' death although he knew that Jesus was innocent. With not a few grave crimes to his own discredit, he most likely let this pass by, without bringing the leaders to justice.

(58) . . . **And the witnesses laid down their garments at the feet of a young man named Saul.**

Even this formality was complied with. Οἱ μάρτυρες, with the article, refers back to the witnesses as already named in 6, 13: μάρτυρες ψευδεῖς. The ἱμάτια here mentioned are the outer robes; usually a long and wide cloth, with bright colored stripes, thrown over the left shoulder and fastened under the right arm; at night the ἱμάτιον might serve as a covering. Naturally garments like this would be in the way when violent movements were to be made. The mention of the person at whose feet they were laid is quite incidental; the laying aside of the garments, however, is a significant formality, although with a great mob of people about, it was natural at any stoning that someone should keep the ἱμάτια. — It was required of **witnesses,** when on their testimony a criminal was to be stoned, that they cast the first stones: "The hands of the witnesses shall be first upon him to put him to death, and afterward the hand of all the people," Deut. 17, 7. A double guilt would thus lie upon a false witness, his perjury, and the murder of the innocent man he himself helped to stone to death. Beginning with verse 54 we have a line of plural participles and verbs which refer to all the people addressed by Stephen, the Sanhedrists, the members of the Hellenistic synagogues, and any others who chanced to be present. They all acted in unison, and so ἐλιθοβόλουν, stoned Stephen. The witnesses with their significant action are not mentioned until this point. We accordingly conclude that in regular order they began the stoning, the crowd after that joining in, until Stephen lay dead upon the ground. — **Saul** is mentioned by Luke for a purpose, the story of the Acts will deal extensively with this man. He is called **a young man,** but this is rather indefinite, since νεανίας, *juvenis,* may mean a man anywhere between 20 to 40 years. Saul was apparently nearer the latter than the former age. The term seems to imply that he was unmarried, to which such other evidence as we have agrees. Some have concluded from the fact that the garments of the witnesses were laid down at his feet, that he must have held some official position in connection with the proceedings recounted by Luke; they suppose that he had been empowered by the Sanhedrim to take action against the propaganda of the Christians. But the basis for this surmise is too slight. This, however, is certain that while Saul himself was not one of the false witnesses, he willingly consented to such witness, for he guarded the clothes of these perjurers. We may properly infer that in the synagogue frequented by the Cilicians Saul, as a Cilician, with the others opposed Stephen, and was worsted like the rest; but just what part he had in securing false witness and bringing Stephen before the Sanhedrim is difficult to determine. He was present, it seems, at the trial, and at least consented to all that had been done in bringing it about. So, finally, we meet him at the stoning of Stephen, and this first mention of his name shows him taking a significant part. Afterwards he himself says of it: "I was standing by and consenting to his death, and kept the raiment of those that slew him." Acts 22, 24. So the guilt for this crime lay upon the soul of Saul just as fully as upon the others. Nor dare we think of anything like remorse or misgivings on his part. In the face of his immediate further action as the prime mover in the "great persecution," especially his voting for the death of other Christians when brought to trial, it is impossible for us to follow those who speak of "the pangs of remorse for Stephen's death among the stings of conscience against which Saul vainly writhed." The notion that he was troubled in the least by his part in Stephen's death, and that any pangs of remorse in his heart were instrumental in bringing him to conversion, is a decided mistake. Saul continued his blind assent until on the way to Damascus the great change was wrought in his soul. — The name **Saul** befitted one who was of the stock of Israel, of the tribe of Benjamin, Phil. 3, 5; it recalled the first king of Israel who was chosen from this tribe. "Circumcised the eighth day," as the same passage states, this old Jewish name was given the boy; perhaps his father bore it before him; and by it he was known in his family and among his Jewish friends. So Luke mentioned this name here. It indeed remained his proper name through life, nor did the apostle afterwards change his name. He had another name from his boyhood on which afterwards for good reasons he employed, thus allowing the name Saul to lapse. Since this name was his as a Jewish child, Christian writers and preachers generally have put a typical construction upon it, making Saul stand for the unconverted man, and Paul for the converted one. But this differentiation is something that others have superadded. — It is an interesting question, whether Saul was in Jerusalem during the time Christ labored in the Holy Land. We know that some years ago he studied here under Gamaliel; it is almost certain that this was before Christ began his work. Where Saul was after that and up to the martyrdom of Stephen we simply do not know. He nowhere even intimates that he met Jesus during the years of the latter's ministry. Olshausen and a few others, in 2 Cor. 5, 16, draw κατὰ σάρκα to Χριστόν, and thus make the apostle say that he was acquainted with Christ while he walked on earth; but this construction is incorrect, and the thought of the passage follows an altogether different line. See *Eisenach Epistle Selections* I, 487. — Saul at this time was one of the most thoroughgoing Pharisees. This was the Jewish party which laid utmost stress upon the strictest outward observance of the Law, and in order to guard it against any possible infraction built up around it a forbidding hedge of traditions and human commandments. Their one aim was to establish thus a perfect righteousness of their own. They emptied out the real inner things of the old covenant religion, and left what remained of the whole only a vain outer show. Their formalism was ostentatious to a degree, especially in ceremonialism, in fastings, almsgivings, the making of long prayers, the paying of tithes down to the tenth part of the smallest garden herbs, and in carrying the most casuistic and painful distinctions into the little details of daily conduct. Yet they were enthusiasts for the glory of Judaism; they "compassed sea and land to make one proselyte." With their national independence lost they centered their efforts in their own hollow way upon the Law and the observance of everything connected with their religion. "It was no longer possible to fortify Jerusalem against the heathen, but the Law could be fortified like an impregnable city. The place of the brave is on the walls and in the front of the battle, and the hopes of the nation rested on those who defended the sacred outworks and made successful inroads on the territories of the Gentiles." Conybeare and Howson. So the people all reverenced them, and even the Sadducees, who scoffed at many things, found it quite convenient to practice many of their requirements. Paul afterwards frequently referred to his blind Pharisaic zeal; "a Pharisee, the son of a Pharisee," brought up in the "strictest sect of the Jews' religion," he writes: "I advanced in the Jews' religion beyond many of mine own age among my countrymen, being more exceedingly zealous for the traditions of my fathers." Gal. 1, 14. And again: "as touching the righteousness which is in the law, found blameless." Augustine's word fits Saul at this stage: "Seek what ye seek, but it is not what ye seek."

(59) **And they stoned Stephen, calling upon the Lord, and saying, Lord Jesus, receive my spirit.**

It is not often that the Scriptures go beyond the simple narration of what they recount concerning Christ and his followers, but here Luke puts in a tragic repetition: καὶ ἐλιθοβόλουν τὸν Στέφανον, adding the name of the martyr with a pathetic touch, and then his first dying prayer. It is again the imperfect tense, holding our attention to the act as at its first mention. — **Stephen** is a Grecian name, στέφανος meaning *crown*, and by a significant coincidence he was the first to receive the *crown* of martyrdom in the Christian church. His Grecian name and the tenor of his speech before the Sanhedrim has led to the conclusion that he was a Hellenist himself; of course, the proof is not really conclusive. His traditional Syriac name is merely a translation, namely *Cheliel* = crown. — Ἐπικαλούμενον is simultaneous with the time of ἐλιθοβόλουν; so we may say, while the stones began to rain upon him he prayed aloud to the Lord. This, as well as the form of his prayer, he had learned from Jesus himself, who when about to die commended his spirit into his Father's hands. Who will recount how many others have followed this precious double example, both martyrs who died for their faith, and others who were not granted such honor? The significance of the prayer is the greater when we recall the vision of Jesus in glory vouchsafed to Stephen at the close of his trial. In the opened heavens he beheld the Son of man, the glorified Messiah, him who was man indeed, but man like none other ever before or after, God in the form of man; and he beheld him on the right hand of God, in the full majesty and power of his glorified state, man still, yet now with all the glory of heaven at his feet; and the vision was of the Son of man "standing," ἑστῶτα, having risen and thus erect, as if he had just risen from his throne of glory to come to the aid of his disciple. To him Stephen now appeals in the face of death. — He uses the address **Lord Jesus,** in all simplicity as when Jesus cried Father on the cross. He who once had walked upon earth as Jesus is Jesus still in heaven. And all that clusters about the name *Jehoshuah* or *Jeschuah* and its blessed meaning "Jehovah is help or salvation" — Jesus, through whom Jehovah effects salvation, — lies in the cry of dying Stephen. This Jesus who has wrought salvation for the world by his death and resurrection will complete his work upon this his dying disciple. — Δέξαι, the strong aorist imperative, refers to a single act, the kind and gracious reception of Stephen's soul as it is about to leave the body in death. Τὸ πνεῦμά μου names the soul or immaterial part of man from the higher side, the side which is able to receive the divine impress and the renewal of the image of God. He who stood aloft, in heavenly glory, we may well imagine, stretched forth his almighty hands ("Father, into thy hands") to receive and conduct into heavenly glory the soul that now came to him. Here is a powerful proof against the lie of Russellism, and all like delusions, which declare death to be the annihilation of the soul; the end of its existence. So an animal dies, its life and immaterial part cease to be; but never the spirit of man. Here again is the clearest answer to the question as to where the soul goes after death: not into an intermediate place, to remain there until the resurrection of the body, but at once to its final abode. The soul of the true believer is received by the glorified Jesus to be with him in his glory until afterwards the body shall follow and likewise enter the glorified state. This is the "building from God, a house not made with hands, eternal, in the heavens," which when the earthly house of our tabernacle is dissolved, shall be ours at once and forever. Comp. *Eis. Epistle Sel.*, on 2 Cor. 5, 1 *etc.,* I, p. 129 *etc.* Those scholars err, and spoil the Christian hope badly, who teach that hades is the receptacle of all the dead until the day of resurrection — hades with an upper compartment called paradise for the souls of the godly, and a lower one, an antechamber of hell, for the souls of the wicked. Beyond a doubt, Stephen's soul went to Jesus in heaven.

(60) **And he kneeled down, and cried with a loud voice, Lord, lay not this sin to their charge. And when he had said this, he fell asleep.** (8, 1) **And Saul was consenting unto his death.**

The δέ is merely transitional, hence the translation "and." Stephen's kneeling was his own deliberate act; he was not thrown down by the stones that hit him. As Besser puts it, a sacred propriety governed his actions. "When he prayed for himself and commended his spirit, he stood erect; but at last, when he prays for his murderers, he kneels down; moreover, he cries with a loud voice, a thing he did not do for his own sake. O how much more serious (since it meant wrestling with God) this prayer came to be for him, than the prayer for himself! How must his heart have glowed then, how must his eyes have melted, and all his body been moved and warmed at the misery of his enemies which he had seen." Luther. The kneeling posture suited both the prayer and the death following so immediately. — Compare ἔκραξεν φωνῇ μεγάλῃ with Luke 23, 46: φωνήσας φωνῇ μεγάλῃ. Here the cry (κράζω) was in imitation of Jesus, as also the prayer itself, which Stephen meant all his enemies to hear. It beat upon the stony ears of Saul, but afterwards when they were opened Paul knew that in himself God had in part answered that prayer. — Κύριε appeals to him who as the true Lord of all shall judge all men in life, in death, and at the last day. For negative injunctions the aorist subjunctive is used; so here μὴ στήσῃς. The verb is used as in Matth. 26, 15: "do not place in the balance for them this sin," *i. e.* to note its weight and thus to charge it against them. Meyer prefers: "do not fix this sin for them." The English idiom is able to convey in either case only the general meaning: **lay not to their charge;** and Stephen's prayer is only a variation of that of his Savior: "Father, forgive them; for they know not what they do." In both cases the prayer asks that God shall not consider the sin final, but shall continue with the work of his grace upon these sinners, if possible to bring them to repentance at last. Neither Jesus nor Stephen thought for a moment of changing God's order of salvation and of his granting forgiveness to men in their wickedness. Both prayers were effectual. In answer to that of Jesus God granted Jerusalem forty years more of the preaching of the Gospel, and thousands were saved. As regards Stephen's prayer Augustine says: "If St.

Stephen had not prayed thus, the church would not have had a Paul; therefore was Paul raised up, because Stephen kneeling down was heard." It is remarkable indeed that a man with Stephen's gifts, though cut off in the first vigor of his blessed work, should be followed so shortly and directly by a man of like gifts and placed in even a higher office. — Having rendered this highest and most precious service to the church, he was now compelled to leave: Stephen **fell asleep,** ἐκοιμήθη; the passive, like the middle, used of lying down, or going, to sleep. Let us note that the word is never used in regard to Christ's death. His death was a different thing, for he died with the curse of all our sins upon him; the Christian dies with this curse completely removed. Because Christ died as he did, we now can die as Stephen died. When his mother named him Stephen she may have thought of some earthly crown or honor coming to her child in after years; the church has given him a fadeless martyr's crown, and the Lord, the eternal crown of glory. The church year celebrates Stephen's victory on the day after Christmas, with this thought: "Yesterday Christ was born on earth, that to-day Stephen may be born in heaven." Sleep is a sweet thing for the tired body; so our bodies at last shall sleep (not the souls), until the great morning of eternity wakes them from slumber. Κοιμητηρία, cemetery, sleeping-place. — Very significant is the addition of Luke (8, 1): **Saul was consenting unto his death;** ἦν with the present participle, the circumscribed imperfect, marks the continuance of the action with special emphasis. The thing was bloody and terrible, but it never checked Saul for a single moment.

Ἀναίρεσις is not just "death" in the ordinary sense; it means putting someone out of the way: murder. This is a flash-light picture of Saul's mind and heart: he was ready to go to the limit of antagonism against Christ. "I verily thought with myself that I ought to do many things contrary to the name of Jesus of Nazareth." Acts 26, 9. Even the possibility that he might thus be fighting against God, as his great teacher Gamaliel had ventured to put it, did not disturb him. One of the terrible things in men's darkened minds is the fullest conviction that they are entirely right when in fact they are entirely wrong. "I did it ignorantly in unbelief," Paul afterwards says; but how desperate and deadly is that ignorance.

(8, 1) . . . **And there arose on that day a great persecution against the church which was in Jerusalem; and they were all scattered abroad throughout the regions of Judæa and Samaria, except the apostles.**

It took the fire of Saul to bring about the first "great persecution." The high priests and others had made various attempts, but all had stopped short; Saul opened the flood-gates. The thing started that very day, for ἐν ἐκείνῃ τῇ ἡμέρᾳ is quite definite. Luke offers no details, but the term διωγμὸς μέγας is very significant; likewise the scattering. But it is providential that an outbreak like this was delayed up to this time. Thousands had been converted in Jerusalem: first the 3000 souls; then the number grew to 5000 ἄνδρες (4, 4); then Luke stops counting and writes merely: "the number of the disciples was multiplying" (61); finally: "the disciples multiplied exceedingly, and a great company of the priests were obedient to the faith" (6, 7). To scatter the ἐκκλησία (assembly, church) now would simply mean to spread it. — The disciples did not at first go far away, only throughout the regions of Judæa and Samaria, many no doubt expecting to return when the fury of the attack had spent itself. This was not cowardice, but Christian prudence, Matth. 10, 23. — On the other hand, **the apostles,** not personally attacked at this time, remained fearlessly at their posts, most likely awaiting their Lord's directions. Besser thinks they waited to gather some of the harvest of Stephen's prayer for his murderers.

(2) **And devout men buried Stephen, and made great lamentation over him.**

Who are these ἄνδρες εὐλαβεῖς? Hardly Christians, but pious Jews, who as such could not well be interfered with by the authorities, if any such thought was in their minds. Compare the term used for these men with Acts 2, 5 and 22, 12. They were grieved at what had occurred; they had something of the spirit of Joseph of Arimathea and Nicodemus who came forward to bury the body of Jesus and also met no interference. There are two traditions as regards the place of Stephen's martyrdom, one that he was stoned beyond the Damascus gate on the north, and another, more modern, near what is now called the Gate of St. Stephen, over against the Garden of Gethsemane. Fanciful legends have grown up about his burial, and portions of his body are said to have been taken to various places afterwards, as relics. Like his Savior he had an honorable burial, and this is enough. The κοπετὸς μέγας refers to the Jewish custom of lamenting the dead by striking (κόπτω) the chest and head, at the same time uttering loud and mournful cries. In this case the Jewish mourning exceeded the usual demonstrations, and shows the esteem of these Jews for Stephen. They were most likely Hellenists, probably the class to which he himself had belonged.

(3) **But Saul laid waste the church, entering into every house, and haling men and women committed them to prison.**

Here δέ marks a contrast; Saul's conduct is the opposite to that of the devout men who buried Stephen. Luke gives only a summary statement, but he uses a strong verb: ἐλυμαίνετο, he continued to ravage, waste, destroy the church — like a wild beast amid a flock of sheep, or some brute in a beautiful garden. This he did by the authority of the Sanhedrim, although the idea of Conybeare and Howson that, perhaps for his energy displayed against Stephen, he was made a member of the Sanhedrim, is certainly without foundation. What authority he had Luke records, and beyond that it is unsafe to go. — Κατὰ τοὺς οἴκους is distributive: from house to house; hence the translation "into every house." The article refers to the special houses, where he expected to make a find. The thoroughness with which this persecutor proceeded is shown further by the participial clause: σύρων τε ἄνδρας καὶ γυναῖκας; both men and women he dragged to prison. This gives a hint of the extent of his depredations among the flock. We must add his own later statements: "I persecuted this Way unto the death, binding and delivering into prisons both men and women." Acts 22, 4, *etc.* "And this I also did in Jerusalem: and I both shut up many of the saints in prison, having received authority from the chief priests, and when they were put to death, I gave my vote against them. And punishing them oftentimes in all the synagogues, I strove to make them blaspheme; and being exceedingly mad against them, I persecuted them even unto foreign cities." Acts 26, 10-11. Even in Damascus Ananias "heard from many of this man, how much evil he did to the saints at Jerusalem," 9, 13. So Stephen had a number of followers in death; how many, and how well they followed the example of his fortitude and love for his enemies the day of judgment will make plain. It was sad in one respect, glorious in another.

(4) **They therefore that were scattered abroad went about preaching the Word.**

The confessors might be bound, the Word was not bound. As the wind scatters the winged seeds of many plants and trees, so the blast of persecution scattered the Word winged by its believers. Stephen was dead, but his murderer had to aid in making the dead martyr speak with a hundred tongues in as many places. It was Luther who praised God by singing at the death of the two martyrs Henry Voes and John Esch in Brussels:

> Naught stops their scattered ashes now,
> Blown out afar to every land;
> In vain is stream, hole, pit, and grave,
> Their foes a poor defeated band.
> Their living tongues by murder crushed
> In death will never now be hushed —
> The world shall hear their singing.

And so (οὖν) they went about — not as they would have planned, but as a greater and wiser mind planned for them. How far they went at last we see in Acts

11, 19. God still directs the cause of his Gospel even in the midst of the greatest upheavals in the church and in the world, and ever the result glorifies his name. In εὐαγγελιζόμενοι τὸν λόγον Luke states the duty of all Christians in all the world. It is only the Word which can serve as such a glad message. All Pharisees hate about it the very thing that makes it so delightful and glorious a message, preaching of grace and pardon for sinners. "The forgiveness of sins is preached in the whole world; which is the peculiar office of the Gospel." *Smalcald Articles VI.*

HOMILETICAL HINTS.

In the line of texts here presented on the life and work of St. Paul the first is intended as a text on human sin and perversion, and the doctrinal trend of the sermon on it will to a large extent be that of the Law. The great sin that lies at the bottom of all the individual sins here shown is unbelief, the wicked and wilful unbelief of the Sanhedrim and others, the blind and perverted unbelief of Saul. The distinctive character of this unbelief is that of work-righteous, self-satisfied Judaism. With this guide it will be easy to follow out the individual sins here described: there are false witnesses, and men who employ them; there is the hypocrisy and self-deception which thinks it protects the honor of God, his temple, and worship by resorting to perjury, false accusation, judicial murder, and general persecution. The Pharisaism which meets us here is only one form of unbelief, but this is akin to all the other forms that have filled the world and that fill it to-day. One of its widespread manifestations to-day is work-righteousness in the churches, which opposes with a thousand lies and deceptions every true presentation and confession of the Gospel of Jesus Christ; besides this, moralism in the world generally, which thinks it enough to avoid some of the coarser sins and crimes and to follow a few "moral principles," say of some secret order, or of other similar teaching, and therefore in all manner of ways opposes the doctrine of sin and grace as laid down in the Gospel. In the Sanhedrim and in Saul we see this root-sin come to full development and flower. It did not always reach this development in those early days, nor does it do so in many cases to-day, but the sin in its essence is always the same, no matter where it appears or what final stage it eventually reaches. The danger and deadliness of this sin, wherever present, and in whatever degree present, should be set forth by the preacher, and the full condemnation of the Law pronounced upon it.

The other side of the text has to do with the Gospel. Here is Jesus himself at God's right hand, the Savior who died for us and now lives and triumphs in heaven; and here is one of his followers who has embraced the full Gospel with all its saving effects, especially also its spirit of love and mercy toward the erring. There lies thus in the text the strongest kind of a contrast: unbelief, all manner of wickedness, centering in the Sanhedrim and in Saul — Christ, the Gospel, faith, and a new life, love, faithfulness unto death, centering in Stephen. But there is more than the contrast, for this text is not the end, with the final judgment to follow, it is a beginning, with much lying between it and the final hour of reckoning. So we must add that all that comes out in Stephen is intended to meet and vanquish all that comes out in his foes, especially also in Saul. This is the synthesis which gives unity to the text, and should do the same for the sermon.

Any kind of false religion, or irreligion, however absurd, is more suitable to the carnal mind than the spiritual truth and worship set before us in the Scriptures. — When we most plainly perceive that men are in the gall of bitterness and in the bond of iniquity, and when we most solemnly warn them of their guilt and danger, we should still exhort them to repent of their wickedness, and to turn to God, if peradventure it may be forgiven.

When a fire breaks out the alarm is rung; when the enemy approaches the signal shot is fired; when danger and persecution come upon the Christian the cry arises: Lord Jesus! Lange.

A man may be highly educated, as was Saul at the feet of Gamaliel; he may even be educated in religious matters to a notable degree; and yet he may be ignorant, blind, erring, groping in darkness, lost. Christ alone is the true light of the soul.

Verbum λυμαίνεσθαι, *vastare, non solum de lupis, ursis, reliquisque feris rapacibus, agros depopulantibus, et pecudes interimentibus dicitur, verum etiam de hominibus.* Rosenmueller.

Just as a vicious dog at his chain, says an old commentator, bites at him who would unfasten the chain, so the ungodly cannot tolerate the touch of those who would free them, they think it a disgrace, and try to rend them. Beloved, even to-day this is one of the saddest effects of the divine Word, when for the obdurate world it becomes a savor of death unto death; when the proud heart will not let the Spirit of God correct it; when the blinded soul can no longer understand the love, the seeking and saving love, that lies hidden beneath the severity of the divine Word; when he who feels himself hit by the preaching of the Word, instead of turning his anger against himself and his sin, turns it rather against the Word of God, as though this were an hard saying, and against the preacher, as though he had offered an insult, yea against the Spirit of God himself, so that the heart is closed the more obdurately against its admonitions. These are the souls that call down the judgment of hardening upon themselves, and heap up unto themselves wrath against the day of wrath. Gerok.

These are still to-day the brutal means by which the world shields itself against the impressions of divine truth. They start an uproar, whether in their saloons or in their newspapers, whether against this or against that preacher of the divine Word, in order to drown the voice of truth. And they shut their ears, in order not to consider the thing and perhaps to be compelled at last to admit: God's Word is right; so as to go on upon their erring way, undisturbed, with blind eyes and deaf ears. Gerok.

The seed of the Word has been dropped into frozen furrows; and when the melting comes it is there ready to spring.

Thus the Word from Stephen's lips dropped into Saul's memory. Arnot.

The early loss of so eminent a minister of Christ must indeed have been a heavy affliction of the church; but how animated was his end, how suited to confirm the faith of the disciples! What an example also were his boldness and tenderness, even for his murderers! The instruction and encouragement of this simple scene might produce the most beneficial effects on multitudes, and that permanently; even far greater than the long continued labors of many eminent ministers. Such in general has been the event of bloody persecution; and the noble army of martyrs has done more perhaps towards the success of the Gospel by their sharp but transient suffering, than the whole company of those who have professed and preached the truth in quiet times.

Stephen's three crowns: the crown of grace with which the Lord adorned him in his life and work; the bloody crown of thorns, which he bore with his Lord in suffering and death; the heavenly crown of glory, which was kept for the faithful witness in heaven. Gerok.

What the Spirit wrought in Stephen: faith and courage; love, patience, kindness, tenderness; hope, victory, triumph. He concluded his sermon and defense by that grandest of all Gospel calls, the prayer for forgiveness, as he sank in death.

The disciples fled; among them many priests. Had they fled through fear of death, they would have taken care not to provoke persecution to follow them, by continuing to proclaim the truths that cost Stephen his life. — One of the fathers has well observed, that "these holy fugitives were like so many lamps, lighted by the fire of the Holy Spirit, spreading everywhere the sacred flame by which they themselves had been illuminated." — A Stephen rose up in every Christian who visited a spot where God's Word had not yet been preached. Stier.

Sleep is a very impressive and appropriate Christian name for death. If we were not made indifferent by familiarity with it, natural sleep would seem a very solemn and mysterious experience. We might well be familiar with death, for we have a symbol and rehearsal of it every night. We might be familiar with the resurrection, for we have a symbol and rehearsal of it every morning. If faith were lively, we might lie down every night as an infant lies down to sleep in a mother's arms: we might be comforted in the morning when we awaken by remembering that this same Jesus stands yet at the right hand of the throne, girt for mighty work, as our protector, and alert to receive all his own, when life is over, into the joy of the Lord. Arnot.

It was a battle when Saul and Stephen met. The latter with his faith in Christ died, the other with his Pharisaic zeal seemed the victor; but the triumph was the Lord's.

When Saul and Stephen Met.

I. *Then the Law met the Pharisee to condemn:*
   1) His black unbelief;
   2) His hollow self-righteousness;
   3) His travesty of virtues;
   4) His hidden and open crimes;
   5) And this, if possible, to produce contrition.

II. *Then, too, the Gospel met the sinner in order to save.*
   1) With its light, and a shining example of faith.
   2) With its offer of pardon, and a shining example of Christian love.
   3) With its hope of eternal blessedness, and the shining example of one who entered it.
   4) And this, if possible, to enkindle faith, and to save.

The Stones that Crushed Stephen.

I. *A symbol of the hardness of unbelief.*
   1) There is no spiritual life and light in these stony hearts.
   2) Their works are all unfruitful.
   3) A cold weight of guilt lies on their consciences.
   4) They are full of stiff and hard resistance to the grace of God.

5) Their stony condition must end in eternal doom, if not broken and removed.
Compare *Formula of Concord* II, 19-23, J. 555.
II. *A monument to the power of faith.*
   1) The Christ who works this faith.
   2) The Word which kindles faith.
   3) The central treasure of faith, forgiveness.
   4) The chief adornments of faith: patience, fortitude, love, peace.
   5) The holy zeal of faith, proclaiming the Gospel.
   6) The eternal crown of faith: glory.

If Saul Were Living To-day.

I. *He might select other forms of unbelief.*
II. *His heart could be altogether the same.*
III. *The Law would smite him as hard as ever.*
IV. *And the Gospel would still be his only hope and help.*

Stephen's End is Typical of the Outcome of Many a Battle between the Kingdom of Light and the Kingdom of Darkness on Earth.

I. *There is often an apparent defeat of the Kingdom of God.*
   1) Stephen dies, and Saul triumphs.
   2) Similar defeats of the Gospel: in the history of the church; in our own experience.
II. *And yet there is always a real triumph of the Kingdom of God.*
   1) Stephen a victor; likewise the others, whose faith proved steadfast.
   2) The Kingdom of God is full of such victories: at the moment of apparent defeat; as a result of such apparent defeats.

Adapted from Lisco.

Saul's Unbelief.

I. *Its root.* II. *Its form.* III. *Its fruits.* IV. *Its judgment.* V. *Its defeat.* (It must either prove its own destruction; or be vanquished by the Gospel against which it fights.)

Who Still Consent to Stephen's Death?

I. *All who persist in unbelief; for Stephen died for his faith in Christ.*
II. *All who cling to self-righteousness; for Stephen died for the Gospel of grace.*
III. *All who stain their lives with sin; for Stephen in death exhibited the finest Christian graces.*
IV. *All who follow false hopes; for Stephen's hope in death was attained.*

THE CHRISTIAN.
Acts 9, 1-9 and 17-22.

Saul's conversion is of paramount interest to the entire Christian Church. Some have placed it next to the death and resurrection of Christ. This is too high, for no man, not even the greatest among the apostles, may approach the Lord. God could have used another man or other men to perform the work he allotted to Saul; he could not have used another to do the work of his Son. But it pleased him to appoint Saul a minister and a witness in a most notable manner for great and blessed ends, and this the church must ever recognize to the praise of God. — Saul's conversion is recounted thrice in the Acts and is variously referred to in the Epistles. In the study of so important an occurrence, and one upon which the Scriptures themselves lay so much emphasis, it will be found absolutely necessary to keep separate the two elements that enter into it. As a sinner Saul was converted in precisely the same way as is every sinner who attains to this experience; Saul was brought to contrition and faith — that is all. Considering this side of it by itself we may say that God might have used any one of a thousand different outward ways for bringing the conversion as such to pass. But there is another side: this man was intended from the very beginning to be an apostle of Jesus Christ, fully equipped and qualified for his high office. This purpose of God explains the special form of Saul's conversion, in particular the direct, visible revelation which Jesus made of himself to Saul on the road to Damascus. Without a revelation of this kind Saul, however truly converted and made a Christian, could not have taken his place as a peer among the other apostles. It would be a decided mistake, then, to mix and confound the two elements here, woven closely together, and to draw conclusions in regard to conversion in general or in regard to individual conversions of others, on the basis of such a mixture. The things that pertain to Saul's future apostleship are altogether exceptional and unique, and as such, though combined with Saul's conversion, have nothing to do with conversions in general. These special features are like the immediate calls of the prophets of old, of the other apostles, and like the special revelations made to them and to others for the purposes of the kingdom. This, too, is the purpose of the divine record of what was thus granted to Saul. In his case, then, we have a conversion indeed, but at the same time much more than a conversion. And thus the praise of God is really twofold: he brought this violent and wicked Pharisee to contrition and faith; and he made this "blasphemer, persecutor, and injurious" "a chosen vessel unto himself, to bear his name before the Gentiles and kings, and the children of Israel." What an astounding work of divine grace! But this is the grace that still works in and through the church to-day.

(9, 1) **But Saul, yet breathing threatening and slaughter against the disciples of the Lord, went unto the high priest,** (2) **and asked of him letters to Damascus unto the synagogues, that if he found any**

Acts 9, 1-9 and 17-22.   41

that were of the Way, whether men or women, he might bring them bound to Jerusalem.

The δέ is transitional, Luke beginning a new account. The insertion of ἔτι connects this account directly with the story as left in the opening verses of chapter 8. Saul had not even moderated his relentless zeal. The description is striking, though brief: **breathing threatening and slaughter against the disciples of the Lord.** The genitives ἀπειλῆς καὶ φόνου after ἐνπνέων follow the verbs of sensation, in particular those of smelling: breathing of threatening and slaughter. The "threatening" for those who could be brought to yield; the "slaughter" or murder for those who remained firm. Note the durative sense of the present participle; we might render it: still continuing to breathe *etc*. His whole inwardness was full of threats and murder, so that he breathed them out in all his actions. And the object of his persecutions were the μαθηταὶ τοῦ κυρίου, *i. e.* of that great and glorious Lord who stood at God's right hand when the heavens opened to reveal him to Stephen. This touch in the narrative helps to bring out the enormity of Saul's sin; it struck at the Lord.
— (2) But the Lord is ready now. Saul has his plans all made to apply more extensively than ever the effects of threat and slaughter; but he plays right into the Lord's hands, his plans shall succeed in a way he never thought. "The Lord God is such a craftsman as has pleasure in difficult masterpieces; then, too, he likes to work in the whole piece. It is for this reason that since of old he above all chose out for himself real hard wood, and hard stone, in order to show his art in the same." Luther. — The question as to who the

high priest was to whom Saul went is beset with some difficulty. It involves the date of Saul's conversion, which seems to have occurred in the year 35, though others place it later. Caiaphas held the office until 36, his successor only one year. But in Acts 4, 6 Luke mentions Annas as the high priest, and in general speaks so of the high priest and high priests that we cannot be sure Caiaphas is meant when he uses the singular. The power and influence of Annas is remarkable all along during the years his son-in-law was the actual high priest. One of the two was appealed to by Saul. — The **letters,** ἐπιστολαί, were credentials and certificates of authority addressed to the Jewish leaders and authorities in Damascus; they were intended to be taken **unto the synagogues** there in connection with which Saul expected to find disciples of the Lord. There is no question but what the authority of the Sanhedrim, and any letters of its leaders, were sure to meet proper response in this as in any other Jewish center. Clark's remark is correct, that in every country where there were Jews and synagogues, the power and authority of the Sanhedrim and high priest were acknowledged; just as papists in all countries now acknowledge the authority of the pope — though without the same justification. — Noesgen reads ἐάν τινας εὕρῃ in the sense of doubt, as if Saul was not sure of finding Christians in Damascus; and imagines that his journey to this place really had some other purpose, the hunting up of μαθηταί being only incidental. But the conditional clause is plainly one of vivid expectation; Saul was sure when he made this move, he was not merely guessing. And the entire description shows that he had but one great purpose in his journey, namely, to hunt the μαθηταί. — **Any that were of the Way** — the genitive τῆς ὁδοῦ expresses quality. The Way itself is not described by an addition; it is the Way κατ' ἐξοχήν, the Christian Way, doctrine, faith, confession, life; ἡ ὁδὸς τοῦ κυρίου, or τοῦ θεοῦ, Acts 18, 25-26; comp. 19, 9 and 23; 24, 22. The Hebrew *derek* is used extensively in this religious or ethical sense in the Old Test.: "the way of the Lord," "the way of evil," "of the wicked," "thy way" or "ways, O Lord," *etc*. The Jews afterwards called the entire doctrine and practice of Christianity *derek hanotsarim*, the way of the Christians. The thoroughness and completeness of Saul's procedure is seen again in the addition ἄνδρας τε καὶ γυναῖκας; he meant to make a clean sweep also in Damascus. The purpose clause ὅπως δεδομένους ἀγάγῃ εἰς Ἰερουσαλήμ shows that the Sanhedrim itself expected to attend to the trial and condemnation of all whom Saul expected to arrest; he was merely their sheriff or constable general. — Why Saul singled out **Damascus,** the oldest city in the world (Gen. 14, 15; 15, 2), is hard to say, except that it was one of the great Jewish centers, and one where Christians were known to be. There were Jews enough in this old capital of Syria that Nero afterwards could put 10,000 of them to death. Lamartine calls it "a predestinated capital," like Constantinople; Eliezer and Naaman the Syrian mark this ancient city for the Old Test. student. Founded before Baalbek and Palmyra, it has outlived both; with Babylon and Tyre in ruins, it is still, in the words of Isaiah, "the head of Syria," and the waves of the Great European war have filled it with modern soldiers and instruments of war.

(3) **And as he journeyed, it came to pass that he drew night unto Damascus: and suddenly there shone round about him a light out of heaven:** (4) **and he fell upon the earth, and heard a voice saying unto him, Saul, Saul, why persecutest thou me?**

The subject of ἐγένετο is αὐτὸν ἐγγίζειν τῇ Δαμασκῷ; note also the present tenses of πορεύεσθαι and ἐγγίζειν. Luke is introducing a notable occurrence, hence the ἐγένετο. But the picture of Saul approaching his goal is such that we are compelled to exclude anything in the nature of an inward preparation due to his past experience. He was in the full swing of his persecution; he was in the act of reaching out farther than ever; Stephen's death and the suffering of other Christians, their testimony and any other Gospel word that had come to him, had glanced off from his flinty heart without making the least rift in its armor. It is for this reason that Saul afterwards called himself the chief of sinners, adding the significant statement: "Howbeit for this cause I obtained mercy, that in me as chief might Jesus Christ show forth all his longsuffering, for an ensample to them which should hereafter believe on him unto eternal life." 1 Tim. 1, 16. Saul was at the climax of his opposition to the Way; it was at this moment that the Lord took him in hand. And Besser's remark is in place: "Let us note well, before we enter upon the miraculous story of our text, that Saul could have considered even the heavenly appearance which threw him to the ground a deception of the devil, if he had hardened his heart against the voice of the Lord Jesus. But God be praised, he was *not disobedient* unto the heavenly vision. Acts 26, 19." — The τε connects the following statement very closely with the preceding. It makes little difference whether ἐκ τοῦ οὐρανοῦ is drawn to φῶς or to the verb, both came from above. Ἀστράπτω is to flash or glare like lightning, and περί means around. The verb is transitive, *umblitzen*. Like a flash it blazed over and around him out of the sky. It may have been momentary, but the conversation following leads us to think that it continued until this was ended. While here only the φῶς is mentioned, verse 17 shows us that this was not merely light, but the light of the appearance of the glorified Jesus himself. This miracle was like the one granted to Stephen, only while there it affected Stephen alone and was full of the most gracious assurance for him, here it affected all present and for Saul was full of the terrors of the Law. "Stephen!" as Besser puts it, Saul's soul may have cried out when he saw the same Jesus and was struck down by his glory. The vision of light was at midday, when the light of the sun is strongest; but it was "above the brightness of the sun," Acts 26, 13, an earthly splendor, such as no created light is able to give. "It was the Shekinah, the glory in which Christ now dwells." *Pop. Com.* Before the simple fact as here recorded and twice repeated in the Acts and variously referred to in the Letters every theory that would offer a natural explanation breaks down utterly. It is ridiculous and absolutely inadequate to speak of a thunder-storm; of a mental phenomenon (how could a flash in Saul's mind throw down all his companions?); of a psychological convulsion superinduced by doubts, remorse and the like. Here there is a direct, miraculous interference by the Lord himself. Saul's eyes saw in that unearthly light, and in its radiance he beheld, the Savior himself. "Have I not seen Jesus our Lord?" 1 Cor. 9, 1; also 15, 8. It was not merely his glory, or the light streaming out from the Savior, but that Savior himself whom he saw. While it is necessary to do what Noesgen insists on, that we note the difference between Acts 7, 55: ἀτενίσας εἰς τὸν οὐρανὸν εἶδε δόξαν θεοῦ καὶ Ἰησοῦν ἐστῶτα κτλ., and here the mention only of φῶς and of no seeing, much less of gazing at what the opened heavens revealed — this difference is accounted for by the persons concerned, whose state of soul was so opposite. But the φῶς is not understood unless we add Ἰησοῦς ὁ ὀφθείς σοι, verse 17; εἶδεν τὸν κύριον, verse 27; ἰδεῖν τὸν δίκαιον; ἑόρακα (Ἰησοῦν τὸν κύριον ἡμῶν), 1 Cor. 9, 1; ὤφθη κἀμοί, 1 Cor. 15, 8. All these expressions require actual *seeing*. The light which revealed Jesus was for Saul's eyes, although it left them blinded; but it was more than any created light, it carried the image of Jesus into the very soul of Saul.

(4) Clark thinks painters are wretched commentators when they picture Saul as fallen from a horse; the fact is, we do not know whether he was walking, riding upon a chariot, or upon some beast, when **he fell upon the earth;** our attention is fixed merely upon his prostrate form — conquered, no longer conquering. The end of his self-chosen way was this place on the road where he lay prone. His attendants were thrown down likewise: "we were all fallen," Acts 26, 14. All through they too are affected, but to a lesser degree. — Now **he heard a voice saying** to him words that were to lead him to contrition, and then to faith. The words were "in the Hebrew language," Acts 22, 14: **Saul, Saul, why**

persecutest thou me? To persecute the disciples was to persecute Christ himself. Augustine: *Caput pro membris clamat.* It is ever so still: Christ identifies himself with his believers; he is the head of the church. Luke 10, 16; Matth. 25, 40 and 45. The words are full of the strongest rebuke; they are the hammer of the Law upon this stony heart which had resisted thus far. Yet they are not the words of judgment, to seal this sinner's doom irrevocably. While they aim at contrition, this contrition is to lead to faith; and so behind the stern tone of the Law there is the intention of grace which tries to save. This comes out fully in what follows.

(5) **And he said, Who art thou, Lord? And he said, I am Jesus whom thou persecutest.**

The question of Saul was uttered as if he then saw Jesus; we must note that the fact of his having been made blind is not recorded until verse 8. So we must say, that until the light ceased, and all was as before, Saul beheld the Lord. His question here has nothing to do with the one whether Saul had ever seen Jesus on earth; there is no evidence that he had. What he utters here is a question of complete surprise, coming out of the ignorance of his soul. He did not know who this heavenly person was. Absolutely sure that he had done God service by persecuting the followers of Jesus, who could this be, shining with unearthly light, and asking why Saul was persecuting *him?* The address κύριε is best taken in a general sense, the only term comporting with the heavenly appearance of the speaker and with the ignorance of Saul concerning his identity. — The answer must have overwhelmed Saul; not merely: **I am Jesus,** but **Jesus whom thou persecutest.** Note the strong emphasis on ἐγώ and σύ, and the contrast between the two. This puny worm of the dust had been persecuting the almighty, allholy, eternally glorious Messiah — Jesus! The repetition of διώκεις has a crushing effect. Could a greater crime be imagined than this persecution of the divine Messiah? But we must not read lightly over the name **Jesus** here used by the Savior. This was the personal name which he bore while he walked on earth, the name he bore as man; he bears it still, for he is still man. His human nature has not been swallowed up in the divine; it has been glorified, participating now completely and forever in the enjoyment and exercise of all the divine attributes of the Son of God. And he is still *Jeschuah,* "Jahveh is help," or "he through whom Jahveh effects salvation" — *the Savior.* All his power, greatness and glory are full of grace and mercy. This Savior-Messiah Saul was persecuting. In his base ignorance he had been fighting both against omnipotence and universal love and grace. What an unspeakable sin! But we must note with care that while Saul's sin went to the full length of its wicked course, in its essence it was the ignorant and wicked rejection of Jesus, the false certainty that he was *not* the Messiah, that he was *not* the Son of God as he had taught, and that all his doctrine was *not* the blessed Word of God and of true salvation. This was the premise from which he drew his fearful and deadly conclusion of persecution unto death. Many are in this very sin to-day although they do not carry their deductions in this direction or to this length. While Saul's persecution was terrible enough, it was the unbelief that deserved the strongest condemnation. All who are like him in unbelief deserve the same condemnation. But here we see also where Jesus grappled with Saul in order to overthrow not merely his wicked zeal, but rather the unbelief from which it sprang: against his false assurances one and all Jesus placed the clear evidence of his divinity and Messiahship. Confronted by this and the power of saving truth that lay therein, the question would now be whether in the soul of Saul this truth would be able to shatter the false assurance which had dominated him thus far, or whether, in the face of this divine evidence and truth, there would rise in the soul of this sinner something new, namely wilful and persistent opposition in spite of all saving influences. The revelation here made to Saul did not work automatically, or with irresistible force; he was not compelled and forced to believe. The truth was stronger than the delusion he had labored under thus far; but man is able to put something else against that truth, something which that truth as it is constituted is not able to crush out — wilful and obdurate opposition, which no truth can conquer. This is what Pharaoh did, *Form. of Concord,* 664, 84-86; comp. 568, 83; 656, 40 and 42. All who do this, either refuse entirely to hear the Word, or, when they come in contact with its saving power, consider it of no account; and thereby "foreclose the ordinary way to the Holy Ghost, so that he *cannot effect his work in them.*" 526, 12. — In Acts 22, 8 the fuller name is given: "I am Jesus *of Nazareth,* whom thou persecutest"; this emphasizes still more the human nature of the glorified Savior. — The A. V. has the addition, omitted by all the best texts: *"It is hard for thee to kick against the pricks.* (6) *And he, trembling and astonished, said, Lord, what wilt thou have me do? And the Lord said unto him."* The first clause is taken from 26, 14, and the rest resembles quite closely 22, 10. Since the words are biblical, although not written by Luke in this place, the preacher may simply let them stand. The first clause is a proverbial expression, variously used by writers in different languages. The reference is to an unruly bullock or ox, to which a sharp pointed stick or goad is applied; instead of moving forward the beast makes an obstinate stand and starts to kick against the goad, driving its sharp point into the flesh. Luther translates: "It *will be* hard," etc., but there is no verb, simply the neuter adjective σκληρόν; and it would be a mistake to refer the saying to Saul's future action, for then he neither kicked, nor was there the prick of a goad. The statement refers to his entire course up to this time, all of it a vain effort and certain only to wound him who made it. It is a terrible thing to turn for oneself the gentle shepherd staff of Jesus into the goad of an ox-driver. Persecuting Jesus could only ruin Saul; it works in the same way to-day. — That trembling and astonishment fell upon Saul is in entire keeping with the occurrence. And the second question is a plain indication that the disobedience of wilful and obdurate resistance was not setting in. This is implied also in the directions which Jesus now gives him.

(6) **But rise, and enter into the city, and it shall be told thee what thou must do.**

The strong adversative ἀλλά breaks off the line of the first thought; it is like saying: I will speak no further of what thou art doing, *but* of what thou shalt do. The Lord might have himself told Saul what to do, but having committed this work to his church and the ministry, he honors both by referring Saul and all men to them. An angel carries Philip to the eunuch, but Philip does the preaching; a vision bids Cornelius call Peter to preach to him the Word. What honor and what responsibility for us preachers, but also what cause for humility and for carefulness in uttering our message! There is grace and kindness in the command ἀνάστηθι, although it is the voice of the Lord. Think what the Lord's power might have done with a persecutor like Saul! He is to go into the city — but not as he had expected to go. There is no compulsion in ὅτι σε δεῖ ποιεῖν; this is the **must** that goes together with the new turn Saul's life took on when he lay prostrate on the roadway. This ὅτι is interesting as the only indefinite relative in an indirect question in the N. T. Blass on this account rejects it, and proposes τί; but Robertson replies with a touch of humor: "Why not call it a 'literary' mark in Luke?"

(7) **And the men that journeyed with him stood speechless, hearing the voice, but beholding no man.**

Not until now are these ἄνδρες οἱ συνοδεύοντες mentioned, and that not so much on their own account, as on that of Saul, who in his blind condition needed their service. The pluperfect ἰστήκεισαν (or εἱστήκεισαν with strengthened augment) has the sense of the imperfect: they were standing. There is absolutely no need of a clash with Acts 26, 14: "And when we were all fallen to the earth" *etc*. This falling was the *first* effect of the light and the heavenly voice; the *second*, that after arising they stood speechless, ἐνεοί. Likewise, there is no clash with Acts 22, 9: "They . . . beheld indeed the light, but they heard not the voice of him that spake to me." Saul saw Jesus in his glory; the men saw no one, only the light while it shone. Then they heard τῆς φωνῆς, "the sound," but not τὴν φωνὴν τοῦ λαλοῦντός μοι (22, 9), the spoken words as Saul heard and understood them. The case is analogous to the one recorded in John 12, 28 *etc*. The two participles ἀκούοντες and θεωροῦντες are intended to explain ἐνεοί, what made them stand speechless and astonished; in 22, 9 there is only the simple record of the facts that they saw the light, but did not hear what was spoken. Just as they saw φῶς, and yet saw μηδένα, so they heard τῆς φωνῆς, yet did not hear τὴν φωνὴν τοῦ λαλοῦντος. The Lord's revelation is only for those for whom he intends it; he knows how to shut others out.

(8) **And Saul arose from the earth; and when his eyes were opened, he saw nothing; and they led him by the hand, and brought him into Damascus.** (9) **And he was three days without sight, and did neither eat nor drink.**

The passive ἠγέρθη is used here in the sense of the middle; the men did not lift him up, he was able himself to arise. The first δέ is transitional; the second, adversative: while he was able to rise, he was not able to see. Ἀνεῳγμένων τῶν ὀφθαλμῶν αὐτοῦ, his eyes having been opened (perf. pass. participle), he was sightless; and ἔβλεπεν, the imperfect, shows that he continued thus. This blindness shuts out all those theories which conceive of the miracle here wrought as an inward thing, transpiring merely in the soul of Saul; such a thing could never make a man blind, or throw other men to the ground, or make them see a light or hear a sound. This outward blindness, however, is typical of the inward condition of Saul. Besser: Now he knew that his soul was blind to the Holy Ghost; his inner condition expressed itself in the condition of his body. He was helpless, and thus pitiable. Others have to lead him. Neither in χειραγωγοῦντες nor in εἰσήγαγον is there a hint of any conveyance or animal to ride; the company may have ridden, but this circumstance is not touched, they may also have walked. — But what a change! He who expected to come as a conqueror, comes now as one conquered. The lion who breathed forth threatening and slaughter, has become a gentle lamb, dependent upon his friends. The fangs of the wolf were broken, his blood-thirst was gone; the terrors of the Law had taken hold of him, his conscience trembled with fear. — (9) This condition continued for three days; the fact of his being blind that long is especially noted. No wonder that thus he **did neither eat nor drink.** This fasting is altogether in keeping with his inner condition; it is the mark of deep contrition and sorrow of heart. Remorse dominated his soul: the thought of Stephen's blood, the blood of other victims, the suffering of the poor captives he had haled to prison, the blasphemy of those whom he had made to abjure the name of Jesus; and most of all, the array of his crimes as a persecution of Jesus, the heavenly Messiah. The exact moment when Saul was converted is nowhere indicated in the Scriptures, and it is in vain for us to try to determine it. Whether the first spark of faith was kindled in his heart by the vision he had of Jesus, or some time during these three days of blindness, or not until Ananias came to him with the words of consolation — who will say with certainty? Nor need we know, either in Saul's case, or in that of any other man. This business of dating conversions exactly is nowhere encouraged in the Scriptures. They show us here only the outward marks of contrition, and in verse 18 his baptism and the further marks of faith. Let that suffice. Prying eyes will never discover the mysteries of conversion, nor the secret processes of regeneration. — — —

(17) **And Ananias departed, and entered into the house; and laying his hands on him said: Brother Saul, the Lord, even Jesus, who appeared unto thee in the way which thou camest, hath sent me, that thou mayest receive thy sight.**

"I am Jesus whom thou persecutest" has the ring of the Law, uncovering Saul's sin and guilt; now for the preaching of the Gospel to Saul the Lord selects a human messenger. The Law indeed drives the sinner to the Gospel, and so Saul had received directions to go and wait in Damascus; but all that is connected with the Law impelling toward the Gospel is not yet the Gospel itself. Ananias, having received full directions, his misgivings all removed, easily finds the house where Saul is, enters it, and finds him. Without hesitation he applies the full comfort of the Gospel to the stricken sinner before him. Let us remember that the Gospel is only for such as he was; often it fails to do its blessed work, because the preparation of the Law has been slighted or done only in part. While we cannot distinguish the inward condition of the soul with due clearness in every case, and in general must preach the Law and the Gospel side by side, the latter always presupposes the former, and we cannot omit the Law unless we do know that its work has been properly done. — We may read ἐπιθεὶς ἐπ' αὐτὸν τὰς χεῖρας εἶπεν: he laid his hands upon him and said. The act is symbolic, not charismatic; it conveyed nothing to Saul, but symbolized what was conveyed to him by other means. This Old Test. practice (Num. 27, 18; Deut. 34, 9) was freely adopted by the apostles and the early church (Acts 6, 6; here; 13, 3; 1 Tim. 4, 4; 5, 22; 2 Tim. 1, 6), and is now used in the same free manner in the rite of baptism, confirmation and ordination. The laying on of hands was especially appropriate because Saul could not see; in effect it was very significant sign language to him. He who had laid hands on others in violence, now has the hands of blessing laid upon his own head. So the Lord rewarded him good for evil. He who deserved the hand of wrath, to smite him with destruction, receives the hand of grace to give him joy and peace. — Σοὺλ ἀδελφέ is in reality a form of absolution. Behind this significant word **brother** there lies what the Lord had revealed to Ananias. "Brother, brother!" how lightly the word is cast about; some preachers are ready to "brother" almost any one. It is too precious a pearl to be thus cheapened and soiled. When did Saul become a "brother," spiritually, by faith in Jesus? We know only that now he is or is becoming such. Ananias properly uses the word since the Head of the church has revealed to him Saul's condition and the divine intention concerning him. — This is clearly brought out in what Ananias now says: ὁ κύριος ἀπέσταλκέν με, Ἰησοῦς ὁ ὀφθείς σοι ἐν τῇ ὁδῷ ᾗ ἔρχου. That same Jesus who had halted the persecutor on his evil way now sends a messenger in order to complete the work he had begun. While the words: **in the way which thou camest** touch the sore spot in Saul's heart, they touch it gently, as does the physician who lays on the healing balm. Out on the road to Damascus: "I am Jesus" had a crushing effect upon Saul, here **Jesus sent me** lifts up and heals. Is. 40, 2; 42, 3. Note ὁ ὀφθείς σοι, and Paul's later identical statement, 1 Cor. 15, 8: ὤφθη κἀμοί. — The blessing which Ananias brings to Saul is twofold: restoration of sight, and the gift of the Holy Ghost. The purpose expressed in ὅπως with the following subjunctives, was, of course, promptly realized. Saul's night of sorrow was at an end; not only were his eyes to see again, but the Holy Ghost would fill his entire soul with the light of truth and faith. It is remarkable how the πνεῦμα ἅγιον (no article, like a proper name) is here mentioned to Saul. The entire Trinity stands forth at once all through the early days of the church. We see the Son appearing in divine glory to Saul, and the Holy Spirit follows this by filling his heart. This presence and gift of the Spirit was attested by many special and marked manifestations, which were granted to that early age alone, and are now withheld. Thus came light, blessing, and power into the heart of Saul.

Acts 9, 1-9 and 17-22.

(18) **And straightway there fell from his eyes as it were scales, and he received his sight; and he arose and was baptized; and he took food and was strengthened.**

Luke loves the little adverb εὐθέως, which he found notable occasions to use. Here it helps to mark the miraculous character of what occurred. It is not well to press ὡς (some have ὡσεί) λεπίδες to mean that an actual substance, some sort of film, fell from Saul's eyes, restoring his sight; Saul rather had the sensation of scales falling from his eyeballs. The entire matter of his blindness and return to sight was miraculous; no further explanation can be given. — Up to this point we have only what had been done for Saul and upon him; now follows his own action, the significance of which is that he had come to faith. Ananias urged him to be baptized, Acts 22, 16: "And now why tarriest thou? arise, and be baptized, and wash away thy sins, calling on his name." Saul needed no long urging, he responded without hesitation: **and he arose and was baptized.** This meant that he confessed his faith in Jesus, which from those earliest times on was a requisite of adult baptism. There is no undue haste here, for Saul knew the Old Test. Scriptures, also the teaching of the Christians, and thus needed but little additional instruction to prepare him for the sacrament. While Luke does not say who baptized Saul, it is entirely proper to assume that this was Ananias. If he was qualified to be God's instrument in bringing Saul the message of pardon and the miraculous return of sight, he was likewise qualified to administer the sacrament, although we know nothing about the position or office of Ananias among the believers. — The Baptists must lay a good deal into ἀναστάς, in order to make out a case for immersion here. While Luke writes briefly and omits the details, this circumstantial participle, used as a matter of course with many verbs, cannot be made to contain a journey to one of the rivers of Damascus in order to have the baptism there. Saul had been sitting in his blind condition; how natural, when his eyes were opened and he was bidden to arise and be baptized, that he should then arise. Ananias does not say, Let us go down to this or that place — river, or pond; or, Arise and let us go down. What he says is that Saul should arise for baptism — and that is exactly what Luke says Saul did. Note also how the baptism is at once followed by Saul's eating and being strengthened. All this looks as if it occurred "in the house of Judas," verse 11, and not as if part of it occurred there, another part elsewhere, and a third part there again. It is impossible to speak in an apodictic way on the mode of baptism either here or in any other place in the New Test.; it seems as if the Holy Ghost, in order to show us that the mode is of no vital importance, left this point veiled in every instance. (Comp. the author's exposition of the different texts in the *Eisenach Gospel Selections,* as well as in the *Eis. Epistle Selections.*) Only one thing stands out clearly, as here, so in other baptisms: immersion is almost, or it is actually altogether, out of the question. While no mode is described, this one mode — as if in anticipation of the perverted Baptist contention — is in various places barred out. — Now Saul took nourishment after his long fast, and revived his fainting strength.

(19) . . . **And he was certain days with the disciples which were at Damascus. (20) And straightway in the synagogues he proclaimed Jesus, that he is the Son of God. (21) And all that heard him were amazed, and said, Is not this he that in Jerusalem made havoc of them which called on this name? and he had come hither for this intent, that he might bring them bound before the chief priests.**

The time embraced in ἡμέρας τινάς is brief: "some days," as we might speak of a week, or ten days, or two weeks. The most tremendous lesson that Jesus himself had taught Saul was that he was indeed the Son of God, infinite in power, glory, and grace. But the μαθηταί, with whom Saul now spent his time, no doubt added a great deal to the details of his knowledge concerning Jesus and the Christian faith. This was necessary for him as a Christian, doubly so for him as the special messenger of Jesus, who would now take up Stephen's work, and presently begin to exceed that greatly. — (20) A second time Luke writes εὐθέως. The energy which Saul had hitherto displayed *against* Jesus, has now found a new channel, and begins to burn *for* him. But there is more in the word, namely Saul's acceptance of the immediate call from Jesus to the apostleship. The story of Saul differs thus from all ordinary conversions. There have been many who thought that when they were brought to Christ they too must at once preach and teach the Gospel; but they lacked the call, also the equipment, their efforts were not orderly, nor was the Lord's blessing upon them in this their undertaking. Saul's example is so far from justifying such believers in their course, that it flatly and roundly condemns it. — **In the synagogues** Stephen had testified, there now Saul takes up the work. Chrysostom writes: οὐκ ᾐσχύνετο, "nor was he ashamed," Rom. 1, 16; Gal. 1, 16: "Immediately I conferred not with flesh and blood." — Luke uses κηρύσσειν, to proclaim as a herald, one of the standard terms for preaching the Gospel; so Saul appeared as a preacher of Jesus Christ, properly called to his great and glorious task. The imperfect tense ἐκήρυσσεν denotes continuance; he made this his constant work. — And the burden of his preaching was: **Jesus, that he is the Son of God;** to which we must add from verse 22: "proving that this is the Christ." This message of Saul to the Jews is the direct outcome of his own miraculous experience; at the same time it is the heart of the Gospel, the quintessence of all godly wisdom. To preach Jesus merely as the son of Mary, to omit or deny that he is the essential Son of God, is to denature the Gospel and to overthrow the Christian religion. The way Luke writes down the message of Saul to these Jews reminds us of Jesus' own solemn declaration before the Sanhedrim, Luke 22, 70. Οὗτός ἐστιν ὁ υἱὸς τοῦ θεοῦ, *he* and none other; *he*, though crucified, for he is risen and at the right hand of God. — No wonder that all his Jewish auditors were **amazed,** ἐξίσταντο, literally: were thrown out of their senses; note the imperfect tense, and the following present participle ἀκούοντες, both durative. And so ἔλεγον, they kept saying, now in one, now in another way: "Is not this" *etc.* The

Acts 9, 1-9 and 17-22.   61

οὗτος is emphatic, though hardly here derogatory. The Jews describe him well: ὁ πορθήσας ἐν Ἱερουσαλὴμ τοὺς ἐπικαλουμένους τὸ ὄνομα τοῦτο, comp. verse 14. Yes, this was he. To call on Jesus' name is to confess him as the Savior, and those who continued in this (note the present tense of the participle) he destroyed. — The clause with ἵνα is in apposition to εἰς τοῦτο; the pluperfect ἐληλύθει is used because Saul's intent had continued in the past, all through his coming, but was done with now. Concerning the former point the Jews, no doubt, had direct information from headquarters, and for the latter Saul was the fullest kind of evidence. This man was a conundrum to the Jews, which they could not solve. And this is true still of all notable conversions; the world has no key in its philosophy that can possibly furnish a proper solution. Only they who have themselves experienced the powers of the invisible world know aright how Saul who once made havoc of the church could now himself build the church. It would seem as if Saul would have been the very man to work among the Jews; we know that God had other and better plans for him.

(22) **But Saul increased the more in strength, and confounded the Jews which dwelt at Damascus, proving that this is the Christ.**

"The Lord humbled him and made him great." Besser. He continued to increase in strength, under the guiding influence of the Holy Spirit and by means of the constant practice his work in the synagogues gave him. This was the inward strength of faith and knowledge, together with the power of utterance in argument and proclamation. — His work was highly effective, although, it seems, only in a negative way: he continued to confound the Jews, συνέχυννεν, upset and rout them completely, and this by his proving, so that none could successfully deny, "that this is the Christ" or the true Messiah. This proof was taken from the Old Test., the Scriptures of the Jews, which they claimed to believe. When Saul showed them what these Scriptures taught concerning Christ, and how all that they taught was fulfilled in Jesus, they were staggered; yet in the face of it all they seem to have persisted in their unbelief.

HOMILETICAL HINTS.

Luke's account of the conversion of Saul is one of the great texts in the Bible, one on which every preacher should feel that he *must* preach at least once. The material, however, is so rich, that there is enough of it for several sermons. In the series here outlined this text will deal chiefly with Saul's conversion, how he became a follower of Christ and was taken into his service; the preacher will deal with the Law and contrition, with the Gospel and faith, with the new life, and with the Lord's call. His task will be to use Luke's account so as to present concretely before his hearers what the Scriptures teach on these great topics, so that their hearts and lives may be touched by the same converting, regenerating, sanctifying, and saving grace of God. "Howbeit for this cause I obtained mercy, that in me first Jesus Christ might show forth all longsuffering, *for a pattern* to them which should hereafter believe on him to life everlasting." 1 Tim. 1, 16.

This is how Buechner analyzes contrition: knowledge of sin; feeling the wrath of God; fear and terror of conscience; humiliation before God; confession of sin; serious hatred of sin. Contrition must continue throughout life, for we sin daily. Contrition has no merit whatever before God; for sin is such an abomination before God, that if a man grieved himself to death over it, he could not thereby atone for his sin. Yet contrition belongs to the divine *ordo salutis,* without which we cannot be saved. The intensity of the sorrow for sin cannot be measured by a definite rule, but depends on the will of God, on the greatness of the moral dereliction, and on the temperament of the person involved. It is a dangerous mistake to force contrition to the verge of despair; its genuineness can be determined only by the outcome, joyful faith and a new life.

"The preaching of repentance which accuses us, terrifies the conscience with true and earnest terrors. In these, hearts ought again to receive consolation. This happens if they believe Christ, that, for his sake, we have remission of sins. *This faith, encouraging and consoling in these fears, receives remission of sins, justifies and quickens.* For this consolation is a new and spiritual life. These things are plain and clear, and can be understood by the pious, and have testimonies of the church, as is seen in the conversion of Paul and Augustine. *Apology,* 94, 62-63.

"But we say that contrition is the true terror of conscience, which feels that God is angry with sin, and which grieves that it has sinned. And this contrition thus occurs, when sins are censured from the Word of God, because the sum of the preaching of the Gospel is this, *viz.* to convict of sin, and to offer for Christ's sake the remission of sins and righteousness, and the Holy Ghost, and eternal life, and that as regenerate men we should do good works." 181-182, 29-30. — "Therefore, such confession is contrition, in which, feeling God's wrath, we confess that God is justly angry, and that he cannot be appeased, and, nevertheless, we seek for mercy because of God's promise." 197, 10. "It does not dispute as to whether there is or is not sin, but it overthrows everything in a mass, and affirms that with respect to us, all is nothing but sin. . . . Therefore, this contrition also is not uncertain. For nothing remains there by which we can think of any good thing to pay for sin, but we only despair concerning all things that we are, that we think, that we speak and do, *etc.*" 328, 36. — The contrition of Peter and Judas is differentiated, Mueller, 169, 10;

182, 36. To that of Judas and King Saul "there is not added this faith."

Faith "is the certainty or the certain trust in the heart, when, with my whole heart, I regard the promises of God as certain and true, through which there are offered me, without my merit, the forgiveness of sin, grace and all salvation, through Christ the Mediator. . . . Faith is that my whole heart takes to itself this treasure." 91, 48. — "Scripture frequently implores mercy; and the holy fathers often say that we are saved by mercy. As often, therefore, as mention is made of *mercy,* we must keep in mind, that *faith* is there required, which receives the promise of mercy. And, again, as often as we speak of *faith,* we wish an object to be understood, *viz.* the promised *mercy.* For faith justifies and saves, not on the ground that it is a work in itself worthy, but only because it receives the promised mercy." 92, 54-56.

"Justificare vero hoc loco forensi consuetudine significat reum absolvere et pronuntiare justum, sed propter alienam justitiam, videlicet Christi, quae aliena justitia communicatur nobis per fidem." 142, 185.

When Saul was raging most against Jesus, Jesus drew nigh to him most graciously. Who can fathom this love? Where sin abounds, his grace abounds still more. Saul pursued Jesus with hate, Jesus pursued him with love.

"Saul, Saul!" — was this to warn this Benjamite that he was following a course like his namesake, the son of Kish? He too had gone out with his men to hunt and hound, and if possible kill, David, the chosen of God.

Why were not the Sadducees, the high priests, the Sanhedrim, the Pharisees converted, like Saul? One answer is, that when the Law brought home their sins to them, they persisted in all their machinations and wickedness, they wilfully hardened themselves against contrition; they seared their consciences.

Let Saul venture to say, Lord, when did we search thee out in thy humble hiding-place, and drag thee before the judge, and witness against thee, and put thee to death? The King shall answer him from his throne. Inasmuch as ye have done it unto the least of these my brethren, ye have done it unto me.

On the repetition "Saul, Saul," comp.: "Martha, Martha," Luke 10, 41-42; "Jerusalem, Jerusalem," Matth. 23, 37; "Simon, Simon," *etc.* This double call always contains reproof and rebuke, at the same time love, pity, desire to help. During the day of grace this continues; but on yonder day there will be no double call.

Why are the shining mirrors in the house of fortune covered with crepe — why is a man taken from the market-places of life into the hushed chamber of sickness and into the long night of pain — why is the sparkling chalice of pleasure turned into a cup of wormwood and gall — why do earthly treasures turn in the hands that hold them to ashes and thorns?

The Word of God is a strange thing. Saul carried hundreds of passages in his mind, but they had not penetrated into his heart. Suddenly that heart was opened — what a flood of light poured in! Let us not despair of constantly teaching and preaching the Word and filling men's minds with it. That Word may seem to slumber a long while. Who knows in how many hearts its power will bring light and salvation at last?

God has woven many a truth into the cloth of our life. We could not read it, or spelled vainly at the words. When the Holy Ghost touched our hearts at last with divine light, the transparency was illuminated, and then we read all that he had written.

The Word, the Spirit, Baptism, the Holy Supper — prayer, confession, a new life, testimony. What wonderful taking and giving!

To be with the disciples of Jesus now as truly one of them means to be with them at last forever — and Jesus in our midst. — In all the world there is no association so precious and profitable as fellowship with Christ's disciples. — Who are your associates?

Saul increased in strength. What folly to think that we need nothing more! Let us not be content with justification, we need as its fruit sanctification; having attained conversion we need daily contrition and repentance; having learned the way of life, we need to know all the power and blessedness of that way. Spiritual sloth is the death of many a believer.

Saul learned what the church was, when he was directed to receive the ministration of Ananias.

The Great Change in Saul's Life.

I. *The Lord found him.*
   1) Saul comes as a foe.
   2) The Lord plants himself in his way.
   3) The Law reaches Saul's conscience.
   4) Saul lies in the dust.

II. *Saul found the Lord.*
   1) Saul sits in blindness.
   2) Ananias comes to absolve him.
   3) Saul is with the disciples.
   4) Saul confesses Christ before men.

How the Lord Conquers the Sinner's Heart.

I. *His mighty arm halts its hostility.*
II. *His divine majesty breaks its hardness.*
III. *His heavenly light illumines its darkness.*
IV. *His forgiving grace removes its guilt.*
V. *His gentle love leads its steps on a new path.*

The Conversion of the Great Apostle to the Gentiles.

I. *It contains the essential features which are found in every conversion.*
II. *It contains certain personal peculiarities which vary in the conversion of different persons.*
III. *It contains extraordinary elements which relate to Paul's apostolate and are not to be expected in any other conversion.*

How the Lord Turned Saul into Paul.

He used
   I. *A penetrating question.*
   II. *A crushing revelation.*
   III. *A gracious call.*
   IV. *A comforting absolution.*

In part from Gerok, *Hirtenstimmen.*

Acts 9, 1-9 and 17-22.

How Saul was Converted.

I. *By grace alone, without any work or merit of his own.*
II. *By revelation alone, the revelation of Jesus Christ in the Word.*
III. *By repentance alone, the sincere change of the heart.*
Naumann.

The Bright Eyes of Faith.

I. *They are blind to the glory of the world, but they see the glory of the Lord.*
II. *They are blind to the hostility of the world, but they see our own past hostility to the Lord.*
III. *They are blind to the ways of the world, but they see the wonderful ways of the Lord.*
Langsdorff.

Saul: Then and Now.

I. *Where were you then?* In the darkness of unbelief.
II. *Who led you hither?* The Savior with his love, his servant, his Word.
III. *What have you now?* A precious possession, a sacred obligation.

In part from Hoffmann.

The Sinner's Conversion to the Lord.

I. *The sinner on his way.*
II. *The Lord on the sinner's way.*
III. *The sinner on the Lord's way.*
K. H. Caspari.

Saul's Conversion a Masterpiece of Divine Grace.

I. *The desperate condition of the sinner.*
II. *The marvelous way in which the Law and the Gospel are brought to bear upon this sinner.*
III. *The astounding result when the work is done.*

THE MISSIONARY.
Acts 14, 1-7.

The Acts contain a number of texts which show us the missionary zeal and skill of St. Paul. In making our choice for this brief series of texts we have passed by the pericopes which have been embodied in the standard lines of texts selected for the church year. Several of these pericopes are among the Eisenach Epistles, notably also Acts 16, 9-15: "Come over into Macedonia and help us"; likewise Paul's work in Philippi, and in Athens. Compare the author's *Eisenach Epistle Selections* II. The aim was to present a new text, and at the same time one in which the chief features of Paul's work appear with sufficient clearness. The text herewith offered measures up to these requirements in an exceptional manner. It appears in none of the tables of texts given by Langsdorff, *Neuere evangelische Perikopen nebst Apostelgeschichte,* where all the different series are found; at the same time it gives us the following essential points: Paul begins his work in the synagogues; it reaches out to the Greeks and Gentiles; he remains until driven out, thoroughly establishing the church; signs and wonders are added; he suffers severe persecution, even the Gentiles joining in; and we may add to our text that somewhere in the neighborhood of these labors he found Timothy and made him his assistant, and on his second missionary journey revisited Iconium and strengthened the church he had so successfully established. The text thus fits our purpose in every way; it shows quite a complete picture of Paul in the midst of his arduous and often dangerous missionary labors.

Paul is on his first great missionary journey; Barnabas is with him, but while at first the latter took the lead in the conduct of the work, this leadership in the most natural way had gradually passed over to Paul. Others were associated with them, Luke writes only οἱ περὶ Παῦλον, "Paul and his company," Acts 13, 1, leaving us in the dark as to the identity of these companions and associates; in Antioch of Pisidia Paul ends up his address: ἰδοὺ στρεφόμεθα εἰς τὰ ἔθνη, "lo, we turn to the Gentiles," showing that his associates are still with him, Acts 13, 46. Our text follows, but mentions no names, not even that of Paul or Barnabas; only the plural shows that the same workers are meant who have been summarily mentioned before. They had been very successful hitherto; "the word of the Lord was spread abroad throughout all the region," Acts 13, 49. While they were forced to leave Antioch, verse 52 reports: "The disciples were filled with joy and with the Holy Ghost." Paul and his companions no doubt shared in that joy. Thus they went on to Iconium.

(14, 1) **And it came to pass in Iconium, that they entered together into the synagogue of the Jews, and so spake, that a great multitude both of Jews and of Greeks believed.**

Ἐγένετο marks a new section, and is followed by the transitional δέ. In later history Iconium has obtained a far more important place than Antioch of Pisidia. It is famous as the cradle of the rising power of the

Turks. It figured as the capital of the Seljukian Sultans. To-day its name is Konieh, and it numbers some 40,000 inhabitants. In Paul's time it was the capital of Lycaonia, although in earlier times the city belonged to Phrygia. Conybeare and Howson draw the following picture: "The elements of its population would be as follows: a large number of trifling and frivolous Greeks, whose principal places of resort would be the theater and the market-place; some remains of a still older population, coming in occasionally from the country or residing in a separate quarter of the town; some few Roman officials, civil or military, holding themselves proudly aloof from the inhabitants of the subjugated province; and an old established colony of Jews, who exercised their trade during the week and met on the Sabbath to read the Law in the synagogue." John Warneck has finely described Paul in the light of present-day mission work *(Paulus in Lichte der heutigen Heidenmission)*; here and in the following pages we will appropriate a few of his statements: "Boldly he presses forward into hostile territory; every success of the never weary conqueror becomes an impulse to cast his net out farther still: Pisidia, Galatia, Asia Minor, Greece do not suffice for him; he must visit Rome itself, and even the world's metropolis is to be only a way-station on his road to the farther west. . . . But his pushing and hastening has nothing unhealthy about it; nowhere is he satisfied with half work. Not until he has established congregations able to live, upon which he may work from a distance, does he move on. It is not his purpose to turn as many heathen as possible into Christians, but he knows that he is called to throw the Gospel as a leaven into the empire, to break up uncultivated soil, to clear the ground, to lay the foundation, in order that others may have easier work (1 Cor. 3, 6 and 10). But with all that Paul is not foolhardy to cast himself with a challenge upon difficulties. As far as we are able to follow his steps we see that he puts forth his strength only where the way is made for him. And this was not everywhere in the Roman world-kingdom. The apostle storms no lands beyond the borders of civilization. He speaks of barbarians (Rom. 1, 14; Col. 3, 11), for whom his Gospel is also intended; but he himself did not go to them. He did his mission work where it would find comparatively the least friction, and where according to the lay of things he might first expect a response. . . . While Jesus preferred to remain among the rustic inhabitants of Galilee, Paul, himself the child of a large city, purposely directs his steps to the cities of importance for the intercourse of the world. In these he gathers his first congregations of Gentile Christians. Considering the active intercourse between the cities, it was to be expected that the seed scattered there would be borne out to many placs." This helps us to understand Paul's work in Iconium. — **They entered together into the synagogue of the Jews, and . . . spake,** means Paul, Barnabas, and whoever else assisted them. There is no disposition on the part of Luke, one of Paul's dearest friends, to magnify the apostle's part in the work, and to reduce that of others. In the previous chapter we have the report of one of Paul's sermons — a sample of his missionary preaching. In the same way he proclaimed the Gospel at Iconium. The conduct of the service in the synagogue permitted the other men to speak likewise; κατὰ τὸ αὐτό modifies both infinitives: εἰσελθεῖν αὐτοὺς . . . καὶ λαλῆσαι = together they entered and spoke; and we see at once, with the very best result. Paul was a strenuous worker himself, but all along we see how he made the finest use of others, thus increasing the fruits of his missionary labors. "The active propaganda of the Jews had successfully paved the way for the Christian missionaries. We know of 150 Jewish congregations along the shores of the Mediterranean during the time of the Roman emperors (Deissmann); and their actual number must have been much greater. When Paul at first turned to these centers of Jewish religious life, he certainly did not intend thereby to make his work easy, but he did it because this method was bound to reach his goal in the quickest manner in entirely strange surroundings. . . . Paul found and gathered together the people in whom he meant to kindle the fire, in order that they might carry it farther. How much more rapidly would the evangelization of the world proceed to-day, if we had a Christian diaspora, centers of Christian life in heathen lands" *etc.* Alas, the "Christian" traders and others who do go to those lands are almost always a hindrance, instead of a help, to the cause of missions. — The emphatic adverb οὕτως is followed by the result clause ὥστε πιστεῦσαι, stating the simple fact: so that a multitude came to faith; so that they did believe. And this was **a great multitude both of Jews and of Greeks;** the genitives are put forward for emphasis. That some of the Jews should believe might be expected; the remarkable thing is that there were many. The addition Ἑλλήνων is still more surprising; so much so, in fact, that Meyer for one thinks he must restrict the term to signify only proselytes of the gate, Greek converts to Judaism who, however, had not adopted all the Jewish customs. But verses 46-48 of the previous chapter show that this restriction cannot apply. These Ἕλληνες, Greeks, were in part, no doubt, proselytes, but the term must include a considerable number of others besides. Nor is this view made impossible by the reference to τὰ ἔθνη in the following verse, for these are the unbelieving Gentiles, and are here placed in opposition to οἱ ἀδελφοί, all the brethren, Jewish as well as Gentile. The occasion when these missionaries spoke in the synagogue must have been one to attract a large number of Gentiles; or the result of the work done there must have spread quickly to include others who heard of it. In general, we may remember, the Jews of the diaspora had begun to do missionary work among the Gentiles, and often with considerable success. While their ceremonial requirements made the thing difficult, and while they often gained only proselytes of the gate, the preaching of Christ, requiring nothing of a ceremonial nature, found hundreds ready to accept it. So here Paul was very successful. — Yet we ought not to press οὕτως here, as Scott does: "*so* plainly, *so* convincingly, with *such* an evidence and demonstration of the Spirit, and with such power; *so* warmly, *so* affectionately, and with *such* a manifest concern for the souls of men; *so* from the heart, *so* earnestly and seriously, *so* boldly and courageously." This is overdoing a good thing — as if at other times and other places, where the effect was not so signal and prompt, Paul did not speak *so*, and *so*, and *so*! The οὕτως cannot be thus separated from its companion ὥστε; the missionaries here spoke *so*, in such a manner, *that* many believed — God blessed their work, they found ready soil. That ought to be enough for this οὕτως. — Here Paul seems to have taken Jews and Greeks in a mass. "But in his proclamation he reached out, like Jesus, preferably to individual souls. In those days, when religious questions were of primary interest, the temptation lay near enough to work upon the broad masses. Forceful speaker and dialectician that he was, the apostle surely would have reaped abundant applause, if he had not just preached the cross of Christ, but had selected what would have gained for him the consent of the finer feelings of the educated. But he scorned mob suggestion. This is always a two-edged weapon, but in religion it is poison. Since in mission work the essential thing is to lead the individual soul back to God, there is no way to success except the one of apparent littleness, the influence of one person upon another. The apostle of Jesus Christ must not scheme to move the masses, he devotes his strength and time to the individual souls of men." Was Warneck thinking of Billy Sunday and his like, and of the entire revival system of the sectarian churches, when he wrote these words? And Kaehler, who writes of the Son of man: "His road unto universalism proceeds through individualism; his road to humanity, through every man." And again: "We think, the road to men proceeds through humanity. The first messenger to the heathen finds his road to humanity, like his Master, through men, through the individual." — These converts **believed,** and the aorist is punctiliar, faith was kindled. This is the one aim and goal of all true missionary work. Whatever else we make, if we produce not believers, our work is a farce, a delusion. Living faith in Christ's blood and righteousness, trust and confidence in him as the Son of God and the Son of man, slain for our sins and risen from the dead, complete reliance upon him for forgiveness, peace, help, and eternal salvation — this is what all preaching, and also all missionary preaching and teaching, must produce. Where this is, all else may easily follow; where this is not, all else may as well remain away, it cannot make up for the vital lack.

(2) **But the Jews that were disobedient stirred up the souls of the Gentiles, and made them evil affected against the brethren.**

Over against the πολὺ πλῆθος Ἰουδαίων τε καὶ Ἑλλήνων Luke, with the adversative οἱ δέ places another class: οἱ ἀπειθήσαντες Ἰουδαῖοι, those Jews who when the Gospel call came to them disobeyed it — this the force of the aorist. They did what Saul once did not do: "O king Agrippa, I was *not disobedient* unto the heavenly vision," Acts 26, 19. "See that ye refuse not him that speaketh," Heb. 12, 25. The sad thing about all preaching, and notably also about missionary preaching, is this, that some become "disobedient," and with salvation knocking at their very hearts, turn to perdition. — Unbelief generally betrays its ugly character; so here: these Jewish haters of the Gospel of salvation by grace through faith **stirred up the souls of the Gentiles.** Just how they did it we do not know; Besser pictures it thus: "We may imagine with what poisonous slanders they were ready; why, of course, the brethren were disturbers of the family peace, men dangerous to the state, secret conspirators, fanatics, and the like." When were the foes of the Gospel ever at a loss for some stone or shaft to hurl against it? And, as when Jesus was to be crucified, Jews and Gentiles readily combine. — The result of this "stirring up" was, **that they made them evil affected against the brethren,** ἐκάκωσαν τὰς ψυχὰς τῶν ἐθνῶν; they embittered their souls, *machten sie boese*, the verb used in this sense only here and in the Septuagint and Josephus. It was, most likely, the usual jealousy that moved these Jews against the missionaries and their adherents; it grieved them to see so many Gentiles come to conversion without first submitting to all the Jewish requirements. So they did what they could to hinder the work. Note the significant name bestowed upon the "multitude" that had come to faith: οἱ ἀδελφοί, they were **brethren** of Paul the apostle and his fellow workers. He was really their spiritual father, but by faith we are all the children of God, and brethren in our relation to each other. Not till later does this incipient opposition focus itself upon the missionaries themselves; at first it is general. God's providence rules among his enemies, so that he provides time and opportunity in the midst of hostility for his messengers to bring their work to a point where they may safely leave it to begin labor elsewhere.

(3) **Long time therefore they tarried** *there* **speaking boldly in the Lord, which bare witness unto the word of his grace, granting signs and wonders to be done by their hands.**

The οὖν goes back over both of the preceding

verses; μέν points to one result, and δέ in verse 4 to another of a different sort. By ἱκανὸν χρόνον is meant a long time in the sense of a sufficient time; it was long enough, considering their purpose. The aorist διέτριψαν is intended to record merely the historical fact; but the following present participles are durative and show what continued throughout the prolonged stay of these missionaries. — By παρρησιαζόμενοι we certainly cannot understand with Clark: "copious and commanding eloquence." Paul as a rule spoke with παρρησία, and wanted the Christians to pray that he might always be able to do so, Eph. 6, 19-20. Παρρησιάζεσθαι is in contrast to ἐπήγειραν καὶ ἐκάκωσαν τὰς ψυχὰς τῶν ἐθνῶν; with the minds of so many "evil affected" against them, they might have been timid and hesitating in what they said. The contrary was true, they spoke with courage and freedom (πᾶς, ῥῆσις), they held nothing back, they spoke openly, caring not who heard them. Warmth, eloquence, *etc.* there may have been, as occasion warranted, but the term used refers to something else and something more important. — This boldness of speech Luke describes as resting ἐπὶ τῷ κυρίῳ, which in spite of Meyer's objections is best referred to Christ. But this basis for boldness is not merely their general confidence and trust in the Lord, that relying on his commission and promise they had nothing to fear; here in Iconium the Lord **bare witness unto the word of his grace** in a signal manner. In μαρτυρέω there lies the idea that the Lord testified that the word which his messengers preached was indeed his word, and at the same time, by the manner in which he bore this testimony, he made it plain who he really was — not a

Jesus dead and buried, his body now gone, no one knowing what finally became of it (this the sham gospel of many to-day!) — but a Jesus risen and glorified, the Messiah in heaven, exercising the divine power and majesty as the great Head of the church. There is no καί before διδόντι, so that this participle describes the manner of the one preceding it (μαρτυροῦντι). — A very precious name is here used for the Gospel: ὁ λόγος τῆς χάριτος αὐτοῦ, **the word of his grace.** It is the word and proclamation which belongs to the grace of the Lord, and χάρις here, as throughout, is the Lord's favor and love shown to those who because of their sin and guilt do not deserve it. The word which this blessed grace uses is its tool and instrument for reaching the sinful and guilty souls of men, in order to bestow itself upon them, free them from sin, guilt, and all condemnation, and make them the children of God. The Word is thus the means of grace. 1 Cor. 2, 1-5. — This Word, which is nothing less than the power of God unto salvation, was worthy of receiving the Lord's own testimony by his **granting signs and wonders to be done by their hands.** It is a mistake to think that the apostles, and others in the early church, performed miracles at will, or whenever they thought it necessary. All the miracles which they wrought were gifts of the Lord; that means that the Lord did not only enable them to perform such wondrous deeds, but that he by his Spirit prompted and directed them when and where to perform them. In this deeper and fuller sense the Lord **granted** or gave signs and wonders; and this granting was not merely a giving to those who were healed and helped by the miracles, it was at the same time a giving to those who by their hands wrought the miracles; and for this they too were deeply and truly thankful. This entire giving was directed by divine love and wisdom: "God also bearing witness with them, both by signs and wonders, and by manifold powers, and by gifts of the Holy Ghost, *according to his own will,*" Heb. 2, 4. The apostles did not always heal the sick, drive out evil spirits, raise the dead; they followed the Lord's will in all these works, as he communicated that will to them. — Luke uses σημεῖα καὶ τέρατα, **signs and wonders;** and we must observe that the latter term is never used alone. "Wonders" are deeds that make men wonder, fill them with astonishment, portents prodigies. Heathen nations all have their τέρατα, and it seems as if the holy writers purposely distinguished the "wonders" wrought by divine power from all such heathen "wonders" by always adding another term or terms. The miracles of the Bible are never mere "wonders" or portents, although even the Jews, who were not satisfied with Christ's miracles, demanded something more of this sort. While any true miracle must produce wonder and astonishment, it is also a sign, it has a spiritual end and purpose. Σημεῖα need not necessarily be miracles; there are many "signs" whose character differs altogether from miracles. But miracles are always "signs," they always signify something. In Iconium they signified that the Lord was present, endorsed the word of his messengers, and was opening the fountain of grace and salvation for all that city and its people. — Διὰ τῶν χειρῶν αὐτῶν does not point necessarily to the laying on of hands, although this symbolic gesture may have been used frequently when miracles of healing were wrought. Warneck: "Paul makes no great to-do about the deeds which God here and there does through him, since he has experienced greater things. He considers them the marks of an apostle, through which God bears witness in regard to his mission work. These undeniably great deeds ... became a divine *attestation* for his life-work and his Gospel. Is it reaching too high, when we expect that divine proofs of power shall render a similar service for the present church in the work of heathen missions?" Warneck answers his question by pointing to wonders that still occur in foreign fields for the sake of the natives there, and by especially emphasizing the wonders of regeneration and renewal among pagan peoples.

(4) **But the multitude of the city was divided; and part held with the Jews, and part with the apostles.**

This is the other result of the work of the apostles and of the Jewish opposition. When Luke speaks of τὸ πλῆθος τῆς πόλεως we incidentally see that Paul's message had penetrated the entire city; the opposition of the Jews had only helped in this direction. Here we catch a glimpse of what Paul's work as a whole must have accomplished. Warneck says, that when we measure this work by what single men achieve to-day, we are astounded. "It is not a rhetorical hyperbole, when Paul says of himself, that he has filled *the world* with his Gospel (Rom. 10, 18; 15, 19; comp. Acts 17, 6)." Of course, he did not bring people everywhere at once to believe in Christ; but this he did do — and we see a sample of it in

Iconium — he established so many radiating centers for the Gospel, that its light soon penetrated all the corners of the different lands. Paul's course from city to city was thus like a triumphal march: "But thanks be unto God, which always leadeth us in triumph in Christ, and maketh manifest through us the savor of his knowledge in every place." 2 Cor. 2, 14. Warneck compares his course of victory with that of Alexander the Great and of Napoleon. What this involves becomes more apparent when we remember that in those days all sorts of exotic religious wares were peddled about; but Paul never failed to arouse the interest of entire cities and districts, some turning against him with hate and violence, others accepting his doctrine or at least giving it tolerant favor. — The division of the multitude of the city at Iconium seems to have been the gradual result of the work of the apostles. The lines were clearly drawn: οἱ μέν . . . οἱ δέ. The original hostility of the unbelieving Jews persisted and formed the center of the opposition. **And part held with the Jews,** ἦσαν σύν, were and continued to be on their side; the other **part with the apostles.** Though Barnabas was not actually an apostle, the plural is here used so as to include him, and we may say also the other associates of Paul. In fact, the word ἀπόστολος is used at times in a wider sense to include other messengers than those who had the immediate call of the Lord like the Twelve and like Paul; thus 2 Cor. 8, 23 and Phil. 2, 25. The Gospel always causes a division, one that at times becomes very sharp and painful. Sometimes Christians do not like this, and the children of unbelief constantly reproach us for bringing about this disharmony, or whatever they may please to call it. But this is the very nature of Christ and the Gospel; he came, not to bring peace, but a sword. Sometimes this divisive power rends families and the ties of friendship, and yet it cannot be otherwise. When light comes, darkness is against it; when righteousness appears, the unrighteous assail it; when life comes, the powers of death bestir themselves to destroy it. Warneck points out that the Gospel, even without becoming polemical, interferes with what the heathen consider their dearest treasures. These people feel instinctively that it is impossible to enter a compromise with Christ. Many heathen religions are syncretistic, but with Jesus there is either the acceptance of faith, or the rejection of unbelief. "Over against the Son of God indifference is impossible; no one can erect an altar for him beside the idols he may have in his pantheon . . . He who is not with him is against him."

(5) **And when there was made an onset both of the Gentiles and of the Jews with their rulers, to entreat them shamefully, and to stone them,** (6) **they became aware of it, and fled unto the cities of Lycaonia, Lystra and Derbe, and the region round about:** (7) **and there they preached the gospel.**

Real persecution finally raised its head. It did not succeed in this instance, but we know what it accomplished in other instances, and how nearly at times Paul forfeited his life. Here was fulfilled what the Lord foretold when he called Paul to be an apostle: "I will show him how many things he must suffer for my name's sake." Acts 9, 16. The general consensus seems to be that ὁρμή must here be taken in the stronger sense of **onset,** "assault" (A. V.), *Sturm* (Luther), instead of inclination or desire, as Noesgen alone suggests. There was more even than a plot; the hostile crowd gathered and started to find the missionaries. The mob was composed of both Jews and Gentiles, together with the rulers of the latter, namely the elders in the synagogue. Some read σὺν τοῖς ἄρχουσιν αὐτῶν as modifying both of the preceding nouns; but this would coordinate and combine in one two very unequal classes: the authorities of the city, and the chief men in the synagogue. It seems altogether probable that only the latter joined the mob, in fact, they may have been the chief instigators of the tumult. This is borne out also by the two infinitives of purpose: ὑβρίσαι καὶ λιθοβολῆσαι αὐτούς — stoning being altogether a Jewish mode of execution. If the city authorities had been active in this affair, they would have had other plans. — In some way Paul and his companions were warned, at least became aware of what was brewing, and fled away (καταφεύγω) to Lystra and Derbe. Their work was done, they could safely leave it behind. Bengel writes: "The refuge of the godly is very roomy — it is both earth and heaven." Paul is prudent, not cowardly. When necessary he risked his life, at other times he did as here, he sought safety in flight. Once a persecutor himself, he is now persecuted himself. But though he fled, he felt no defeat; he merely left one victory behind to start winning another. — He followed the roads to the southeast, seeking this time less populous places, it seems in order to avoid clashing again with the Jews. All that we read in the following section concerning Lystra deals only with Gentile superstition, and nothing whatever is said about Jews. Among the very noteworthy things about Paul is his ability to accommodate himself to the Gentile world. When we remember his exclusive Jewish training and life up to full manhood, this ability of his to enter into the life and thought of the great Gentile world becomes the more remarkable. How almost completely he laid aside the peculiar Jewish mode of thinking and reasoning and followed one that would put him into closest touch with the people of the Greek world, his Epistles show. The story of his missionary work as recounted in the Acts shows us the same thing. This too he did by the grace of God, and became thus once more a model for those who come after him. Lystra and Derbe, however, were again to be only centers of missionary influence; καὶ τὴν περίχωρον, "the region round about" is significantly added. This general on the firing line is always and ever a strategist, and every new position that he occupies he utilizes for his military purposes to the utmost. The circumscribed imperfect, ἦσαν with the present participle εὐαγγελιζόμενοι, is even more expressive of duration than a simple imperfect would be; hence we conclude that Paul again spent some time in this territory, preaching the Gospel — than which there is no work in the world grander, more satisfying, and more beneficent.

HOMILETICAL HINTS.

The sermon on this text, as the author contemplates it, is not to be a mission sermon of the kind preached usually at mission festivals. The preacher will keep to his theme Saint

Acts 14, 1-7.

Paul, and make his hearers once more come into contact with this great Christian personality. Only, this time it will be Saint Paul the missionary, the devoted, tireless, courageous, masterly, successful herald of the Gospel among Jews and Gentiles. It will be well to keep to the idea that Iconium gives us only a glance at this side of the great life of St. Paul; something of what lies beyond may be added, but the rest must be left for the hearer himself to supply — his imagination having been given proper direction. As far as the cause of missions is concerned, the effect of the sermon will be the greater the more the preacher does justice to the character of the great apostle as here shown in the full swing of his work. When something of the fire that glowed in his bosom is kindled in the hearts of us all, there will be no lack either of workers for the field, or of supporters of the work at home. In general we may say, it is not enough to shoot off a few heavy mission guns when we have our annual mission festivals; to be sure, we want good, strong, stirring sermons then; but we want more — the steady fire of love for the Lord's cause, which utilizes his Word all along to arouse and increase interest in his great work. Paul is the greatest missionary that ever lived — his example a gift to the church of all the ages. For our people to know this man is to receive impressions that cannot but be fruitful in many ways.

"The Word of God must be preached everywhere to the very ends of the earth, until sinners thrust it from them; and Israel's God still in all times and in all places stretches out his hand to the people, who gainsay it instead of listening to it, after he has so long endeavored to dispose and prepare these sinners for eternal life. He in his longsuffering only declares them unworthy of it, when they have filled up the measure of their sins by driving away his messengers." Stier.

Who needs the Gospel? Let us ask rather: Who does not need it? Every man who is *like the Jews,* self-righteous, self-satisfied, attached to any wrong religious notions, whatever they may be, sure that all is well with him, and that he needs no more. Every man who is *like the Gentiles* — and the world is full of them even in our so-called Christian lands. These are the men who are proud of human nature and who speak of Nature with a capital letter; who love the world and the things that are of the world, especially the things that gratify the senses, that flatter the mind — a little philosophy, a touch of cheap science, amusement, the theater, the dance, passionate lovers of games, festal occasions, the tinsel of parades and uniforms, and the bonds of secret orders which furnish these and other things adapted to the flesh, not the least of which are indulgences of the carnal appetites. Surely, all these need the mighty regenerating power of the Gospel.

Assuredly, the Lord is able to use as missionaries only people who truly believe in him, truly love him, truly follow him. But such people we all by right ought to be, and should therefore not look upon mission service as an extraordinary service. G. Warneck, *Missionsstunden* I, 9. — Some of the following paragraphs are from the same source.

Missionary Rebmann worked for 29 years at a lonesome post in East Africa; he saw but little fruit, lost his health, even the sight of his eyes, and finally returned home. To this man an English friend of missions once spoke of the sacrifices he thus brought. But the missionary indignantly replied: "What are you saying — *sacrifices?* One never makes sacrifices in the service of the Lord. He sacrificed himself for us; but when we serve him, it is only grace, and even if we suffer in his service, it is grace." Thank God, this is the thought of many missionaries. But it would be very fitting for the friends of missions at home, who have given to the work not even a son or a daughter, but only a few dimes and dollars, also to think thus.

The thing that makes mission work so unpopular, yea, hated, is its preaching by word and deed so positively from the housetops the doctrine of the Scriptures: "There is no salvation outside of Christ, the Lamb of God, which taketh away the sins of the world." Like no other work of Christian saving love mission work has written on its banner *"The Word of the Cross,"* and this Word is still an offense to the Jews of modern days, and foolishness to the Greeks of the twentieth century.

Arnot writes: When the community is dead in sin, to throw the word of life into the stagnant mass necessarily disturbs it. Although the Redeemer is the Prince of Peace, he is not satisfied with the serenity of a dead sea. He casts in a solvent whose nature it is in the first instance to arouse and separate. The peace which he values is the purity which is reached through conflict. People must take sides when the cross of Christ is preached in time, as they must take sides when the throne of God is set in eternity.

It is not so difficult even among large masses to arouse a feeling of pity in regard to bodily needs, for instance in the case of a famine which destroys thousands, or in the case of a flood, or a mighty conflagration, or the sufferings which follow in the wake of war. In all cases of this kind we may count on a certain natural feeling of pity. But the thing is entirely different when help is needed to relieve spiritual destitution. Then the natural feeling of pity will not suffice, then only the people who have fixed their hearts upon eternity, are the ones upon whom we can count. Since mission work is a work which rescues for heaven, it demands as workers men whose love goes beyond time and things temporal. If you then are unable to warm up your heart for this work, it is because your love lacks the proper length, that is because it does not extend to eternity.

In almost all cases the heathen are very unlovely people, and treat the messengers of Christ precisely as did the Jews Christ himself: "He came unto his own, but his own received him not." There is little romance connected with mission work.

With soldiers who have lost hope the best general will win no battles. Our Lord Jesus will and must conquer at last. If we believe that he has all power in heaven and earth, this must make us joyful in hope and confident of victory. Or have we, amid the difficulties of the work and the opposition of the foe, lost faith in the victory of Jesus and in the saving power of the Gospel? It almost seems so at times, when we see the discouragement of the faithful and hear their constant complaints.

Those who refuse to obey the truth often proceed to turn others from it. "Ye entered not in yourselves, and them that were entering in ye hindered." Luke 11, 52. . . . The world might quietly allow people who would like, to be converted unto the Lord. What would it hurt? Why should not others have what they themselves in their pride reject? But their conscience testifies that it is the kingdom of heaven which they reject, that they are spurning a heavenly treasure; their conscience makes them jealous and determined that others shall not see that the Gospel is a treasure, and pick it up, and become rich by possessing it. Willinger.

The Lord has means enough to stop the mouths of his enemies. When the Jews succeeded in casting suspicion upon the word of the apostles, new works, signs and wonders, were granted unto them, done before the eyes of all the world, a preaching by deeds to the Gentiles who had been stirred up.

A word of justice could only terrify and condemn; a word of learning could only affect the intellect, and the higher the learning the less possible its attainment for men generally; a word of law and command would only add to the weary load already upon the sad shoulders. Nothing but the divine Word of grace, of pardon and forgiveness, of regeneration and a new life — nothing but this Word is of avail in a world full of sinners.

Iconium:
St. Paul in the Midst of his Mission Work.

I. *His field* — Jews and Gentiles — alike in darkness, sin, death — alike in need of forgiveness, life, and salvation — a hard field — but one to which the Lord led him.

II. *His means* — the Word of grace — how exactly it fits the needs of the sinner — with absolutely nothing able in any way to compete with it — St. Paul's reliance upon this Word — his constant application of it.

III. *His special aid* — Barnabas and others — the prayers of the church which had sent them all out — the hand of providence — signs and wonders.

IV. *His opposition* — disobedient Jews — slander and vilification — Gentiles who allowed themselves to be evil affected — but Paul counted on all kinds of opposition — he could

not be defeated — though he avoided persecution when his work was practically done.
V. *His success* — it came quickly here — it always came — it was signal, a congregation was formed, and it was in a neighboring town that he found Timothy.

St. Paul an Inspiration for Mission Work.

I. *His clear vision.*
II. *His complete devotion.*
III. *His tireless zeal.*
IV. *His noble courage.*
V. *His marvelous success.*

With one of the Lord's Generals in the Forefront of Battle.

I. *The foe.* II. *The armament.* III. *The tide of battle.* IV. *The spoils of victory.*

The Greatest Work in the Word.

I. *Its range:* Jews and Gentiles.
II. *Its means:* The Word of grace.
III. *Its task:* The creation of faith.
IV. *Its result:* Eternal salvation.

The Divisive Power of the Gospel.

I. *Though the Gospel has salvation for all men alike,*
II. *And all men alike are in dire need of salvation,*
III. *Only some men yield to its saving power,*
IV. *While the rest obdurately reject it.*

The Drama of Faith and Disobedience.

I. *It is enacted in men's souls,*
II. *When Christ meets the forces of sin and death,*
III. *With the saving Word of his grace,*
IV. *Which some accept in faith,*
V. *And others reject in wilful disobedience.*

THE PREACHER OF JUSTIFICATION.
Rom. 3, 20-26.

Christ our Savior and all his apostles preached justification by faith, even as did the prophets of the Old Testament. Justification is the central doctrine of all the Scriptures, the heart and soul of the entire Christian religion. All believers are justified, all the saints in heaven now have been made what they are by justification, and at the last day the righteous at Christ's right hand will be there because they have continued in justification to the end. It was given to Paul in a notable way to set forth the doctrine of justification and to defend it against all the forms of work-righteousness current in his day. Thus by the grace of God this apostle became for the Christian world of all ages in a special manner the preacher of justification and righteousness by faith. Two of his Epistles deal with this doctrine in an extended manner, namely Romans and Galatians. It is impossible to preach properly on St. Paul without preaching at least one sermon on some part of his presentation of this glorious doctrine. Naturally we here select as choice and rich a text as we can, one out of the heart of the great Epistle to the Romans. In the first part of this Epistle St. Paul sets forth that all men, Jews as well as Gentiles, since they are all and altogether sinful, need the salvation in Jesus Christ; thereupon he shows that righteousness and life is received alone by faith in Jesus Christ. The opening verse of our text is part of the closing argument on the sinfulness of all men and their inability to reach righteousness by means of the Law. In what follows Paul describes how God has prepared a righteousness outside of and apart from the Law, a righteousness which is made ours by faith. This is the direct exposition of the great theme he announced in the first chapter, verses 16-17. Besser sums up the contents of our text as follows: Without merit, by grace; without help of the Law, through faith, or as Luther succinctly expresses the apostle's meaning: by faith *alone*. The efficient cause of salvation is the grace of God alone; the meritorious cause, the atonement through Christ's blood alone; the apprehending cause, faith alone. By this doctrine of righteousness God is properly honored as the God of a righteous people, gathered from among the Jews and the Gentiles, and among this people of his grace the Law is not abolished, but properly established.

(20) **Because by the works of the law shall no flesh be justified in his sight: for through the law** *cometh* **the knowledge of sin.**

We begin our text with this important verse which really closes the argument in regard to the Jew's lost condition, as far as anything the Law can give him is concerned. The Law was indeed a great and glorious possession; it distinguished Israel above all other nations; yet it was a vain hope to think that the Law could save the sinner. It could— and can — do nothing of the kind. All it can do is to stop every mouth and bring all men under the judgment of God. But how is this? $\Delta \iota \acute{o} \tau \iota = \delta \iota \grave{\alpha} \ \tau o \hat{\upsilon} \tau o \ \ddot{o} \tau \iota$, *propter hoc quod*, **because** — because all the works done in the effort to meet the requirements of the Law fail to justify a man. And why so? Because the Law, when we give close heed to it and its requirements, shows us that we have not met these requirements, that it is impossible for us to meet them; because the Law reveals to us our sin. — **The Law,** ὁ νόμος, is the Mosaic Law, as it was given to Israel; not merely the ceremonial law, or some other legal regulations of the people of the old covenant, but the entire complex of divine Law which God had given them, the essential part of which is known as the moral Law, to which Paul also makes special reference, 2, 18 and 21 *etc.*, also 26 *etc.* We may say that the ceremonial and civil parts of the Law, as the Jews had them, were detailed specifications and applications of the great inner moral principles of the Law, as these details were best suited for the purposes of God in dealing with Israel. But these inner moral principles of the Law were themselves of universal application to men; Paul speaks of them as they applied to the Gentiles who had no outward form of this Law given to them; and we to-day feel the same constraining force of this inward part of the Law, its moral principles and requirements. — **The works of the Law,** then, are all those works which the Law requires, which men attempt to render in order to meet its requirements. We may say that there are two general classes of such works: those performed by the unregenerate; and the good works of the regenerate. The latter indeed are ἔργα ἀγαθά, or καλά, but they always remain imperfect, and thus prove insufficient for justification. Much lower are the works of the unregenerate, whose efforts at living up

to the Law fail in the most vital parts, the inward things of the fear, love, and trust of God. Paul, however, does not specify here, he simply lays down the rock bottom truth: "By the works of the Law shall no flesh be justified in his sight." The preposition ἐξ indicates origin or source: from this source justification will be obtained by no man. Gal. 2, 16.
— **No flesh,** πᾶσα σάρξ with οὐ (δικαιωθήσεται), is used in the sense of οὐδεμία σάρξ, or οὐδείς, no man; not even an Abraham, or Peter, or Paul, or any other saint, to say nothing of others. The allusion is to Ps. 143, 2, where David wrote the equivalent of πᾶς ζῶν (LXX): "for in thy sight shall no man living be justified." There is no direct quotation, only an appropriation of David's thought and words. We need not press σάρξ to mean man in his sinful condition, or man in his bodily frailty; it is enough that the term refers to man as a human being. Whatever works of the Law any man thinks he has, or even actually has, they can not justify him. — Δικαιωθήσεται, **shall be justified,** has the well known sense of this verb in the New Testament and in the Scriptures generally: to declare just. **In his sight,** ἐνώπιον αὐτοῦ (αὐτοῦ for the direct σου of the Psalm), does not mention the judge as an agent, but the judge as one in whose presence the culprit stands. Nor is it correct with Stoeckhardt to erase the passive sense of the form here used and make it read: "will *become* just"; his idea that ἐνώπιον αὐτοῦ favors this is quite inconclusive. The future tense is here used in a general way: shall be justified at any time, whenever appeal is had to God and his judgment. Philippi calls it the future of moral possibility, or an abstract future. While the last judg-

ment, at the end of the world, is not shut out in any way by the form of the word, it is also not especially referred to here. Let a man bring all the works of the Law he can possibly gather together, and present them before the face of God at any time, the moment the divine δίκη or norm of right is applied to these works, there will result, not a declaration, that they measure up to this norm, but the very opposite. The expression ἐνώπιον αὐτοῦ we think suggests that when these works are brought into God's sight they lose the beauty they may have had in the sight of man; in his presence they appear as what they really are, the bulk of them totally evil, and the best of them altogether inadequate and insufficient. No man is able to show a perfect fulfillment of the entire spiritual Law of God; no part fulfillment will answer. — Paul now, in a way characteristic of him, reverses his thought. He turns the coin over, for it has two sides. If the works of the Law are unable to bring us the sentence of justification, it is because they deserve the sentence of condemnation. **For through the law** *cometh* **the knowledge of sin.** The γάρ furnishes a reason; and it is this: these works cannot justify, because when examined by the Law they show no righteousness to correspond to the Law, they show the opposite — sin, ἁμαρτία, a missing of the divinely set mark. The very Law to which the man who brings the works of the Law makes his appeal, when he seeks to secure from the divine Judge the sentence of justification, reacts in the opposite direction, it reveals his sin. By ἐπίγνωσις is meant a deep knowledge, a knowledge that really knows. Paul here merely states the fact; but there is divine intention behind it. For God knew that among fallen men no one could measure up to his Law, and yet he gave that Law. Did he mean, then, only to condemn all? We know his purpose was a blessed one: to work the knowledge and conviction of sin by the Law, in order that the Gospel might follow with the gift of the forgiveness of sin. "Here there is a hard clash between man who is a condemned sinner and wrestles with death and fears every moment to be cast into hell, and God whom he has insulted and angered. If the sinner here is not to despair and die in his sins, a better mediator than Moses must appear, namely Christ the Lord himself, to satisfy the Law, remove its wrath, and be able to reconcile the condemned sinner, worthy of eternal death, with God." Luther. "We unanimously believe, teach and confess that the Law is properly a divine doctrine, wherein the true, immutable will of God is revealed as to how man ought to be, in his nature, thoughts, words and works, in order to be pleasing and acceptable to God; and it threatens its transgressors with God's wrath and temporal and eternal punishment. For as Luther writes against the Antinomians: 'Everything that reproves sin is and belongs to the Law, whose peculiar office it is to reprove sin' (Rom. 3, 20; 7. 7); and as unbelief is the root and spring of all reprehensible sins, the Law reproves unbelief also." *Formula of Concord,* J. 592, 17.

(21) **But now apart from the law a righteousness of God hath been manifested, being witnessed by the law and the prophets;** (22) **even the righteousness of God through faith in Jesus Christ unto all them that believe.**

Here Paul begins the second part of his letter. With the Law failing to justify, and all men left under judgment, the Law itself only confirming it by showing their sin — what hope and help is there for man? Here the apostle lets the Gospel speak forth and tell the very sweetest part of its story. **But now,** νυνὶ δέ, cannot be taken in the temporal sense (Philippi), as if Paul had spoken thus far of the times before Christ, and now would speak of the Christian era; there is instead a logical turn of thought, the line of negative argument: οὐ δικαιωθήσεται, receives a positive counterpart: δικαιοσύνη θεοῦ πεφανέρωται. It is a sad, dreadful chapter that ends with verse 20; but that was the necessary preliminary and background for the glorious, delightful chapter which now follows. — **Apart from the law,** χωρὶς νόμου, is in direct contrast to διὰ νόμου of the previous verse; and Luther translates finely: *ohne Zutun des Gesetzes;* without aid or cooperation of the Law. The Jews who had the Law and prized it so highly were absolutely sure that all righteousness before God depended on the Law. Paul himself had thus been intent as a Pharisee to set up his own righteousness by means of the Law. This old Pharisaic notion seems to be part of our old Adam himself, for always and everywhere men are inclined to seek some sort of righteousness by works of their own in the Law, either the one given by God, or one which they manufacture themselves. They will not see that this sort of righteousness is of no avail in God's sight. "But now" the wonderful thing is, with all Law righteousness altogether unavailing, that there should be another righteousness, one really availing, and this — "apart from the Law." It does not grow out of the Law, and the Law never did a thing to produce it, nor does the Law now give it. Note the emphatic position of χωρὶς νόμου at the head of the sentence; the phrase, however, modifies the verb, and not its subject: this new and wonderful righteousness of God has been revealed, and thus stands revealed now before us all, outside of the Law. — It is significantly called **a righteousness of God.** It is a righteousness of the Gospel, not of the Law. And right here let us note: that the Law always demands without giving; but the Gospel always gives without demanding. This "righteousness of God" here cannot be the essential attribute of God, his holiness and righteousness; for this would be revealed already by the Law which demands on the part of a righteous and holy God that we on our part live up to the requirements of his Law. The genitive θεοῦ denotes origin indeed, for this is a righteousness wrought entirely by God, and not by men; but at the same time it is one which avails before God: *die vor Gott gilt,* Luther. Here again we must hold fast the forensic meaning involved in δικαιοσύνη; this is a righteousness which consists in a declaration made by God the Judge. — The wonderful thing is that this righteousness **hath been manifested,** shown forth, made manifest, and the perfect tense πεφανέρωται implies that having been revealed it is now continuously open and manifest to all. This implies that men in themselves never knew nor could know this righteousness; also that the Law could not reveal it unto them. Stoeckhardt and Zahn both argue that since this righteousness is made manifest, it must have existed before being thus manifested; they do the same with the

7

statement Rom. 1, 17: δικαιοσύνη θεοῦ ἀποκαλύπτεται, "therein (in the Gospel) is revealed a righteousness of God by faith unto faith." The former finds this righteousness existing in Christ, who was made unto us righteousness, 1 Cor. 1, 30; and the latter finds it existing in a sentence of forgiveness pronounced by God upon the entire world of sinners declaring them all to be righteous. Now Christ is indeed our righteousness, namely Christ in his atoning merits, but only as we apprehend him by faith and thus have the declaration of righteousness pronounced upon us. In 1 Cor. 1, 30 the apostle does not speak of Christ our righteousness objectively, but as he is apprehended by faith and thus becomes our righteousness in subjective possession. Likewise it is true that God accepted Christ's merits as sufficient for the whole world of sinners, and mightily declared this by raising the crucified Christ from the dead; but it is not true, as Stoeckhardt claims, that God thereby actually forgave the sins of all the sinners in the world, and that this is what the righteousness of God signifies, and that this is now what is revealed or manifested. In Rom. 1, 17 it is a very serious mistake to overlook the addition ἐκ πίστεως εἰς πίστιν; and in our passage verse 22: δικαιοσύνη θεοῦ διὰ πίστεως Χριστοῦ, εἰς πάντας καὶ ἐπὶ πάντας τοὺς πιστεύοντας. The righteousness of God is not merely the merit of Christ as he wrought it out for all men; or the sentence of God accepting this merit as sufficient for all men (much less the impossible, unbiblical thing, that God in advance justified every individual sinner in the world and every one yet to come into it!) it is God's sentence of forgiveness and justification pronounced upon faith in

Jesus Christ: "unto all and upon all that believe." Paul is speaking of *imputed* righteousness. "Therefore," with our entire Lutheran Church, "we believe, teach, and compass that our *righteousness* before God is, that God *forgives us our sins* out of pure grace, without any work, merit, or worthiness of ours preceding, attending, or following." *F. C.*, 501, 4. In a very pregnant sense this is the righteousness *of God,* since all that belongs to it: Christ and his merits, faith and the apprehension of these merits, as well as the justifying imputation and declaration is all θεοῦ, God's very own. And that such a thing as this could at all be no man on earth could ever have figured out; God himself had to reveal it by the Gospel (Rom. 1, 17) and make it manifest "by the law and the prophets." The Gospel is indeed a mystery from the foundation of the world, but one which it pleased God to reveal and make manifest unto men. — **By the law and the prophets** = by the Old Test., the popular Jewish designation for which was "the Law and the prophets," or adding yet a third member: "and the other books." The apostle could here have quoted Old Test. statements to show how the Old Test. bore witness concerning this righteousness; he reserves that for chapter 4, where he speaks at length of Abraham and quotes from David. Here he aims to show only that this wonderful "righteousness of God" is nothing totally new, novel, or strange, without historical background in past revelations; while made manifest apart from the Mosaic Law with its demands, and thus in a certain sense the opposite of this Law, still the Old Test. contained this righteousness. **Being witnessed,** μαρτυρουμένη, pres. tense, witnessed all along.

Do you ask how? In many ways. The old covenant as such was the promise of a new covenant; the beginnings of the Gospel and God's great Gospel plan are in that old covenant; it is full of types, promises, prophecies of the Messiah. All this part of the Old Test. "witnesses" God's righteousness, bears testimony — one that we hear still when we go into the Old Test. — that God justifies all those who believe. Since no man was able to be justified and saved by the Law in those olden times, the way of salvation then was as now: by faith alone. Bengel: *Lex stricte* (χωρὶς νόμου) *et late* (ὑπὸ τοῦ νόμου) *dicitur.*

(22) The theme of Paul's entire letter is δικαιοσύνη θεοῦ, hence here, as he enters upon the positive presentation of it, he emphatically repeats the essential words, using δέ to help mark the emphasis: **even the righteousness of God.** But this repetition left bare as before would make no progress, hence the additions which bring out fully now what Paul's great theme really is: **even the righteousness of God through faith in Jesus Christ unto all them that believe.** The whole statement belongs together and must be taken as one; to cut it up, and to speak of faith by itself, and in the same way of those who believe, is to misconceive and misinterpret the apostolic words, and that in a matter of the very highest importance. Neither δικαιοσύνη nor θεοῦ have the article, and so the phrase διὰ πίστεως is attached without putting ἡ before it; the connection is so close that we could almost use the German *Glaubensgerechtigkeit* for it. This righteousness of God, instead of being ἐξ ἔργων νόμου, something dependent on our efforts, is διὰ πίστεως, a righteousness **through faith,** and thus truly a righteousness of God,

not one based on our efforts. We will understand the noun δικαιοσύνη in this connection when we note the force of the verb: δικαιοῦσθαι διὰ πίστεως, as in verse 30 and Gal. 2, 16. The righteousness of God is present only where God pronounces the sentence of righteousness or justification. Speaking abstractly, not yet concretely of men or any particular class or individual, this righteousness is present where faith is present, or more fully: **faith in Jesus Christ.** Πίστις and πιστεύειν is divinely wrought trust and reliance upon Christ as the Savior from sin and guilt; the genitive Ἰησοῦ Χριστοῦ is objective. This explains the διά: God's righteousness is mediated by faith in Jesus Christ. The Christ embraced by faith always makes ours the divine declaration of justification — and this is to have God's righteousness. Or, to begin at the other end: God's righteousness, which always implies his judicial declaration: I declare righteous! is found only where faith is, faith relying on Jesus Christ and his merits. The idea that God's righteousness exists in some way by itself, that it is then revealed and manifested, and then faith appropriates it and makes it its own, is a perversion of Paul's teaching, and of the blessed truth which he taught; a perversion which should be impossible in the face of our Lutheran confessions where this matter is made so exceedingly plain. The δικαιοσύνη θεοῦ exists only διὰ πίστεως, never apart from it and merely waiting for faith. Apart from faith there is nothing but the sentence of condemnation, the κατάκριμα θεοῦ, and no δικαιοσύνη θεοῦ with hope and expectation that unbelief will yield at last to faith. — Paul now gives the thought which he has thus far kept in abstract form, a concrete turn:

unto all and upon all them that believe. The textual authority for the words καὶ ἐπὶ πάντας is so good that this emphatic repetition should be retained. Note how the apostle piles up prepositions to show as fully as possible what he means: διά — εἰς — ἐπί. The phrase διὰ πίστεως, which is abstract, is elucidated by the appositional phrases: εἰς πάντας καὶ ἐπὶ πάντας πιστεύοντας. Here we have actual believers: πιστεύοντες, those who are believing, continuing to do so. And εἰς and ἐπί connect with these concrete persons what is always connected with faith, or let us say mediated by faith — the δικαιοσύνη θεοῦ. Where faith is there God's righteousness is; and this means: where believers are there is God's righteousness. As it is διά faith, so it is εἰς believers and ἐπί; it is mediated by faith, divinely wrought faith, and that means that God's righteousness, which rests on his justifying declaration, goes out to all believers, and comes down from above upon them — πιστεύοντας, the moment they believe and as long as their believing continues. And the double, emphatic πάντας would have us mark that not a single believer is here excluded, every one by being a believer, by having faith, by trusting in Christ, has, not a righteousness of his own, but one God himself has prepared for him, one that counts with God, one which rests on his own judicial finding, and which this Judge will always and everywhere acknowledge. And this is how the righteousness of God is revealed in the Gospel (Rom. 1, 17), and testified to by the Law and the prophets of old: they all show and proclaim that a poor sinner is justified before God by grace through faith in Christ. The δικαιοσύνη θεοῦ exists actually only in believers, and it is their distinctive quality; but they have not produced it, they have only received it, it is imparted to them by a divine declaration of God in heaven, a declaration that goes out to every man in whose heart God sees Jesus Christ received by faith.

(22) . . . **For there is no distinction;** (23) **for all have sinned, and fall short of the glory of God;** (24) **being justified freely by his grace through the redemption that is in Christ Jesus.**

The apostle inserts γάρ, for he is now beginning a line of proof to elucidate and establish what he has just said concerning God's righteousness by faith in Jesus Christ. The proof begins with a fundamental statement denying that there is any διαστολή, **difference.** If one had in mind only the immediate connection, he might think that Paul refers only to the πιστεύοντες he has just spoken of; but this narrowing would be quite arbitrary. "For there is no difference" is axiomatic and general. The one difference that might be thought of here is that between Jews and Gentiles discussed by Paul in the first section of his Epistle. This, of course, is barred out when it comes to the δικαιοσύνη θεοῦ; and so is every other that one might care to mention, difference of age, of sex, of social position, *etc*. There is no such difference, not merely among those believing at that time, or at any time, but actually among all men in general so far as righteousness and justification are concerned; neither nationality, age, sex, or anything else gives any man an advantage, helps in any way before the Judge who determines the righteousness of faith as present or absent. — (23) So also the next clause, which substantiates the fact that there is no difference, by pointing to the essential likeness. **For all have sinned,** that shows (γάρ) that there is no difference. Zahn, and Stoeckhardt restrict πάντες to the πάντας τοὺς πιστεύοντας of the previous verse, as though this new πάντες takes up the previous one. They point also to the following participle δικαιούμενοι, as though this referred back likewise to the πιστεύοντες who have the righteousness of God. But Meyer is right when he points to the present tense of this participle; if the believers in verse 22 were meant, Paul would have written an aorist participle. He is discussing universal truths: there is no difference between men in general; all men have sinned (not merely all believers of Paul's day); and for all of them justification comes freely *etc.* The use, then, which we constantly make of this passage as a proof for the fallen condition of our whole race is justified. Πάντες is absolute. — And all ἥμαρτον, 2nd aorist, **have sinned,** really: did miss the mark; the historical aorist records the simple though terrible fact. Luther writes: "They are all sinners *etc.* is the chief article and central passage of this Epistle and of the entire Scriptures." It is chief in a negative way, for God's whole plan of salvation was made to match our fall into sin. — The thing is emphasized and expressed more fully by the addition: καὶ ὑστεροῦνται τῆς δόξης τοῦ θεοῦ. To come behind is to **fall short** and thus miss altogether, as one who remains behind in a race; ὑστερεῖσθαι thus pairs well with ἁμαρτάνειν. — The genitive τοῦ θεοῦ with τῆς δόξης names the author: "fall short of the glory or honor which God accords." Philippi takes δόξα τοῦ θεοῦ in the sense of ἐνώπιον τοῦ θεοῦ, or παρὰ τῷ θεῷ, which is practically the same, though the genitive strictly speaking does not have this meaning. God's own essential glory cannot be meant here; nor the glory of heaven; nor the divine image in which man was created; nor is δόξα = καύχησις, which Paul would have used, had he desired it. The Apology uses our passage: "The righteousness of reason does not justify us before God, and does not fulfil the Law, Rom. 3, 23: 'All have come short of the glory of God,' *i. e.* are destitute of the wisdom and righteousness of God, which acknowledges and glorifies God." (88, 31).

(24) All men have missed the mark, all now are left out of the race (ὑστεροῦνται, pres. tense); as far as they and their efforts are concerned they are all lost. But thanks be to God who meets this desperate condition with his grace! **Being justified freely,** δικαιούμενοι δωρεάν, is really the chief thought of the sentence, although only a participle — the Greek lending itself to such constructions, as Philippi well remarks. The statement thus receives a peculiar force: the action of the participle accompanies the action of ὑστεροῦνται. It would change this thought to read δικαιούμενοι = καὶ δικαιοῦνται. They all fall short of the glory of God while they are justified freely; or, while thus falling short, they are justified freely. Justification, a divine act sets in, where their own effort and act leaves them utterly lost. The participle, however, is not intended to say that all men now are actually justified. Besser has Paul's thought when he says: "Gospel justification finds as miserable sinners all to whom it comes, and clothes in its garment all the destitute sinners upon whom it comes. Here we see how far the promise of the Gospel extends: as far as sin extends, over the whole world; and according to

Melanchthon's admonition we are to arm ourselves with such universal terms — as "all" — against the false notions of predestination." They who take πάντες as referring to πιστεύοντας in verse 22 thereby have a restriction for δικαιούμενοι; though one would expect, that since they were already mentioned as believers, and also since their faith was expressely referred to, here we would have the aorist participle: all (these believers) *having been* justified. Paul's thought is entirely general; he is not considering that some will not believe, but only that the way of justification is open to all who by their sins fall utterly short of acceptance and commendation by God. It is hard to see why the passive sense of δικαιούμενοι should be given up in our passage, as Stoeckhardt for instance insists: *"becoming righteous."* Δικαιοῦσθαι and other passive forms, also passives of some other verbs, are frequently used intransitively; but the passive sense remains in many other cases. So here both English versions very properly retain it and translate: "being justified." When Zahn, however, urges the intransitive meaning of the passive δικαιοῦσθαι for the purpose of eliminating from all such forms the forensic idea of being declared just by a judge, substituting the general notion of divine help in "becoming" just, he is mistaken and leads astray. Cremer settles this matter as far as the language side is concerned; see his *Bibl.-Theol. Woerterb. d. Neutest. Graezitaet*, 10th ed. by Jul. Koegel, on the Hebrew *zadak, hizdik, etc.*, the classics, the LXX, the Apocrypha, and all the writers in the New Testament. The latter always use or imply a personal object. Always δίκαιος is: just in the judgment of God; *"der Gottes Ur-*

teil fuer sich hat." Δικαιοῦσθαι = to become just, and δικαιωθῆναι = to be just, but both only in this sense: *"das Urteil Gottes fuer sich haben,"* to have the *judgment* of God in one's favor. The matter is summed up in the following statement: "This meaning of the passive is the less a proof against the forensic sense, since everywhere it is plain that the relation meant is one in regard to God's judgment, and since δικαιοσύνη in Paul's language, just as in the Scriptures otherwise, never signifies an accomplishment or a virtue, but a *relation* to God's judgment, and δίκαιος one who has this *judgment* in his favor," p. 328. All Zahn's remarks about our Lutheran forefathers who held fast so firmly the forensic meaning of all the forms of the word here in question, thus fall by the side; these good old fathers fully understood Paul, while Zahn does not. Even Stoeckhardt's remarks on the intransitive sense of the passive are insufficient and do not properly clear up the matter, although he uses Luther as his support. Both for Luther and for the word itself more must be said, as we see in Cremer. — So in δικαιούμενοι, **being justified,** there is an agent implied; and if we translate: *"becoming* just," or: *"becoming* righteous," the sense dare be only: just, *in the judgment* of God; just, so that he *declares* us just. The agent, namely the divine Judge, remains behind the word, and must remain, unless the sense of this and other most precious passages is to lose a vital element. — Being justified **freely,** δωρεάν = gratis, for nothing, by way of gift, likewise implies an agent, namely a giver. This δωρεάν shuts out all human merit of whatever kind. When God declares a man just, or when he becomes just, is justified (passive) — this is wholly and in every part without his having produced, furnished, or brought anything before God, which the judgment of God could accept. Not the least particle of δόξα or credit can he obtain by anything of his own. The most subtile synergism is here barred out. But when some understand that faith also is shut out, that unless it were also barred, synergism in some form would result, they only show that they fail to understand faith, this blessed work of God, not of man. So little is faith barred out, that it is always and everywhere included; and no justification of any sinner ever takes place except by faith. The Scriptures are full of this δωρεάν; Rom. 5, 17: ἡ δωρεὰ τῆς δικαιοσύνης; Eph. 2, 8: θεοῦ τὸ δῶρον; comp. Matth. 10, 8; Rev. 21, 6; 22, 17 for the use of δωρεάν.

(24) **By his grace,** τῇ αὐτοῦ χάριτι, shows how "freely" is meant. One of the most comforting words in all Scripture is this latter word χάρις, grace. It signifies the divine favor and love as something altogether undeserved by him to whom God extends it. "Mercy," ἔλεος, is God's favor or pity toward those who are miserable and wretched under sin. Thus the χάρις is always first and fundamental, and ἔλεος follows; strictly speaking this order cannot be reversed. In τῇ αὐτοῦ χάριτι, instead of τῇ χάριτι αὐτοῦ, the αὐτοῦ is put forward for emphasis; this is lost in the English translation, which is unable to give such an emphatic position to "his." It is *God's* mercy, over against all human mercy, which brings about justification. And this idea of mercy goes together well with the forensic sense of δικαιούμενοι, for grace implies a person who is gracious; if the great Judge should follow only his

righteousness and the righteous claims of the Law against the sinner, he would condemn, and not justify; but he is moved by grace. — How this can be when he, as every just judge must judge justly, is shown by the further modifier: **through the redemption that is in Christ Jesus,** the redemption connected with him, or bound up with him as the Messiah who saves ("Christ Jesus"). Ἀπολύτρωσις is redemption in the sense of release bought by a λύτρον or purchase price; war captives, slaves, *etc.* were thus ransomed. In the less distinct use of the word the idea of a purchase price was lost, and the word was used in the general sense of liberation, release. But the specific meaning is retained throughout where redemption is spoken of in connection with man's release from the curse and penalty of the Law, the judgment and condemnation of God, and his justification before God. This is seen in the synonyms that are used: ἀγοράζειν, 1 Cor. 6, 20; 7, 23; ἐξαγοράζειν, Gal. 3, 13; περιποιεῖσθαι, Acts 20, 28; λυτροῦσθαι, Tit. 2, 14. Especially instructive are Matth. 20, 28 and Mark 10, 45, where Christ speaks of giving his life as a ransom, or λύτρον, for many; also 1 Tim. 2, 6, "who gave himself a ransom, ἀντίλυτρον, for all." Thus in our passage there follows the mention of "his blood," as that which effected our ransom. The grace of God is able to justify because it has the means necessary for this purpose. We of ourselves would be forever lost, but another comes and lays down a sufficient price for us; and this the great Judge is able to accept. Christ's redemption is the meritorious cause of our justification. In διά the thought of means is expressed; God uses Christ's λύτρον to outbalance our guilt, the ἀπολύτρωσις in Christ to cancel our bondage under sin and its curse.

(25) **Whom God set forth** *to be* **a propitiation, through faith, by his blood, to shew his righteousness, because of the passing over of the sins done aforetime, in the forbearance of God.**

The ἀπολύτρωσις is so vital for God's justifying act that he adds a fuller description, specifying more closely what Christ our Redeemer did by describing what he himself was in the doing. **Whom God set forth** — he the actor throughout; and προέθετο, the historical aorist. This verb as Cremer-Koegel point out, is a cultus term, one used of things relating to the tabernacle and Jewish worship. It is almost technical, and fits exceptionally well for the connection with ἱλαστήριον. In a solemn and holy manner God "set forth" Christ; and this for himself, as the middle voice implies. — For **a propitiation** Luther has *Gnadenstuhl,* "mercy-seat," which takes ἱλαστήριον in its true sense, namely *Kapporeth,* the term used for the lid of the ark of the covenant in the tabernacle. One meets strange things in studying the work of commentators. A man like Zahn spurns this signification of ἱλαστήριον by calling it an ancient notion which even at present is not quite dead — and this he does in the face of the fact that Delitzsch, Tholuck, Cremer-Koegel, Meyer, Ebrard, Philippi, Stoeckhardt, Besser, and a host of others hold to this meaning, and reject the one Zahn himself offers, namely the general term *Suehnmittel,* "means of expiation." The term τὸ ἱλαστήριον is a neuter substantive from the adjective ἱλαστήριος, which in turn comes from ἱλάσκομαι, to make propitious, to reconcile, to propitiate by expiation. The LXX gave the word that specific, almost technical meaning, which Paul here used for Christ in his atoning work. It is superficial for Zahn to take the *Kapporeth* in the sense of *the place* where expiation was made, so that, if the word were applied to Christ, the counterpart could only be the wooden cross on which Christ hung and which his blood stained. Christ himself is a ἱλαστήριον or *Kapporeth:* as the cover of the ark was spotted with the blood of the atonement, so was Christ covered with his blood shed on the cross; as this blood-stained cover covered up the tables of the Law lying beneath it in the ark, so Christ bloodstained covers up the Law and its accusing commandments for us. Every Jew knew from the LXX what this term meant, and outside of Judaism the LXX was widely known. "To set forth as a mercy-seat" shows what God did for a sinful world in order to enable him to pardon and justify; and both terms used are solemn, sacred, exceedingly impressive. Our English versions have only the very general term: "propitiation," and the margin of the R. V. even tries to make it a mere adjective: "propitiatory." This is surely unfortunate.

The two modifiers: **through faith, by his blood** belong to ἱλαστήριον. Christ is to be a mercy-seat "through faith." The divine intention is that we believe in him, that thus he as our propitiation may avail for us, and God justify us. — **By his blood** completes the thought of the mercy-seat. By means of the blood sprinkled upon it the ancient Kapporeth was so effective for Israel; so is Christ our mercy-seat now ἐν (in or with) τῷ αὑτοῦ αἵματι — the αὑτοῦ in the emphatic position: *his* blood, *his* alone. — The following phrase: εἰς ἔνδειξιν κτλ, shows the divine purpose which God had in regard to himself in thus setting forth Christ as a mercy-seat: **to show his righteousness,** to demonstrate and declare by a public act. And here δικαιοσύνη αὑτοῦ can refer only to the essential attribute of God, not as in verse 20 to a righteousness intended for us. That God is a Judge full of righteousness in all his dealings is shown by what he did with Christ, setting him forth before all the world on Golgotha as the propitiation for the sins of the whole world. In Christ our Substitute all our sins were punished, and when now for Christ's sake God pardons the sinner he is a just Judge and righteous in his act. This he shows; men are to see it; but what he shows is something in himself. It is important that men see it; but it is far more important that God have it in himself. The divine righteousness demanded a *satisfactio,* an expiation; without it there could be no justification, acceptance, or help for the sinner. — Paul says that God made this demonstration of his own righteousness in the bloody propitiation of Christ **because of the passing over of the sins done aforetime, in the forbearance of God.** This is lifting out a part from the whole, namely the sins committed before Christ's sacrifice was made. The ἔνδειξις is for the world, surely not for the Jews alone, and so "the sins done aforetime" are best taken as the sins of all the world done before Christ. These God had passed over; πάρεσις is *prætermissio, neglectio,* allowing them to pass; it is not ἄφεσις, *condonatio,* forgiveness. The passing over implies a future reckoning; to pass over without that would be the opposite of righteousness. This was due to **the forbearance of God,** his ἀνοχή or patience. He endured these sins, he did not bring them promptly to final judgment. God looked forward to Christ's atonement, and when the fulness of time was come, on account of these sins (διά with the accusative) he displayed his righteousness in laying them on Christ our Substitute, the Substitute also of all who had lived before. Heb. 9, 15 speaks of the Jews: "for the redemption of the transgressions that were under the first covenant." Acts 17, 30 speaks of the Gentiles: "The times of ignorance therefore God overlooked." God indeed punished in the time before Christ, but only in a limited manner. His righteousness was not fully vindicated until Christ died on the cross. — (26) **For the shewing,** *I say,* **of his righteousness at this present season** emphatically repeats the chief point in the previous statement, adding the specification of time up to which the forbearance extended and with which it reached its conclusion. Now the forbearance of God need not thus exercise itself, since Christ's blood covers all sins to the end of time. This phrase with πρός some connect directly with πάρεσιν, instead of making it epexegetical to εἰς ἔνδειξιν; the sense is practically the same in either case. — **That he might himself be just** *etc.* sets forth the purpose God had in all that he did with Christ in a still more general way. He was concerned about demonstrating his righteousness as regards the world before Christ; but his intention goes beyond that in a grand manner, including that indeed, but embracing the whole world, mankind of all ages. God is concerned about himself: that he might himself be δίκαιος, righteous and just in his own judgment. It is his own righteousness which demands atonement and expiation for sin; in Christ God satisfied this demand. — **And the justifier of him that hath faith in Jesus,** δικαιοῦντα, "the one justifying," pronouncing the verdict of acquittal; τὸν ἐκ πίστεως Ἰησοῦ, him who is of faith (supply ὄντα), means every one whose character is marked by faith, who from faith as from a fountain or source has what marks him. God justifies only the believer; but in doing so he is himself just, for the believer, though a sinner and as such worthy of condemnation, as a believer has Christ and his propitiation, and for Christ's sake God can, yea, must justify him. It is a grave error to change what Paul here says to mean that God justified the entire world of sinners in accepting Christ's atonement, and that now men only need to believe this. The justifying act takes place in heaven for each believer individually, the moment God's Spirit enkindles faith in his heart. This, and nothing other, is our precious evangelical Lutheran doctrine of justification by faith. Let us thank God for this glorious *sedes doctrinæ* for which he used the heart and pen of St. Paul!

HOMILETICAL HINTS.

St. Paul is great as a man, as a Christian, as a missionary, as an orator, as an organizer, *etc.,* but he is greatest by far as a divinely inspired preacher and writer on the doctrine of justification by faith.

No man who fails to understand sin can understand Paul's preaching of justification by faith. There is a Pelagius in us all, and sometimes he blinds whole generations to their sin, in order to darken their eyes for grace. But Paul and Pelagius are opposites. Let the apostle of God's righteousness kill out in your heart every notion of a righteousness of your own, no matter who the Pelagius that gave it to you.

To Christian believers, enlightened by the Spirit of God through the Word of Scripture, the entrance of which giveth light, it is amazing that ever so many who desire to be enlisted among Christians are carried away by the speculations of science and philosophy to notions which leave them without God and without hope in the world. The outlook in that direction is one of despair. But God still lives and his Word abides. There are still some, no thanks to the preachers of natural evolution and progress and social improvement, who feel the misery of sin and seek relief from its crushing burden. Loy, *The Augsburg Confession,* 477.

Man is magnified, and the grace of God is minimized; little account is made of human sin, that the more account may be made of human virtue; great account is made of human power, that less account may be made of divine grace; stress is laid upon human merit, that the merit of Christ may seem less: in short, man is exalted and the glory of God is proportionately diminished. Loy, p. 476 on the error of Rome, which is found all over the world also outside of Rome.

The sense of law which attempts to work out salvation for itself, whether it have a superficial color or be full of self-tormenting honesty, always ends in the bankruptcy of the religious life. It never brings God nearer; for it can produce nothing but transgression of the law. At best it shows only ideals which remain unattainable. No Chinese is able to live up to the doctrines of virtue taught by Confucius. No India penitent finds the desired peace. No serious Mohammedan is able to follow the contradictory commandments of the Koran. It is a simple fact, that the religions which say so much about works and aim to gain the divine favor by virtue, never attain their ideals. The honest confessors among them admit this . . . they offer God a coin which he cannot accept. J. Warneck, *Paulus,* 307.

It is by far another thing: to do the works of the Law — and to fulfill the Law. Luther. Also: The Law does nothing but reveal sin and make it alive, which before the knowledge of the Law lies dead and slumbers.

If Moses had not written of Christ (John 5, 46), the joy and heartfelt delight in the Law, which from the first Psalm on in the entire book of Psalms sings its songs, would be incomprehensible; but because the saints of the old covenant by faith lifted themselves up above the Law in Christ, the hard yoke of the Law became gentle for them, its harsh voice lovely, its "thou shalt," bitter as gall, a honey-sweet "thou canst." As often as the righteous in the Psalms and the prophets comfort themselves with God and are comforted in God, the righteousness revealed in the Gospel is witnessed, which the Law cannot bring forth, yet has imaged in a silhouette, which the coming Christ cast before him. Besser.

There is no difference: there are not several ways of becoming righteous before God, but only the one, the way of faith; not two plans of salvation, one for the Jews and respectable people, and one for the Gentiles and publicans, but one for all, for the virgin Mary and for the malefactor, for Paul and for the emperor Nero. And for this reason there is no difference as to becoming righteous, because there is no difference in being sinners: for they have all sinned. Besser.

If God had desired only to be righteous on his part, and not at the same time to enable us to become righteous, he would have punished sin at once in full severity, and not have provided an expiation for it in Christ Jesus. Daechsel.

Faith is not a human notion and dream, which some think it to be. But faith is a divine work in us, that changes us and regenerates us, *etc.* Luther, *Preface to Romans*.

God passed over the sins done aforetime — also those in which you lived in ignorance and religious indifference. Dryander's application Acts 17, 30.

Luther writes: "I had (1519) in truth a hearty desire and longing really to understand St. Paul's Epistle to the Romans, and nothing had up to this time hindered me, save only the little word *justitia Dei* in chapter one, verse 17, where Paul says that the righteousness of God is revealed in the Gospel. I was very hostile to this word 'God's righteousness,' and was advised and taught according to the manner and

custom of all teachers in no other way than that I must
understand it in the philosophic manner of a righteousness in
which God is righteous for himself, does and works right, and
punishes unrighteousness in all sinners; which righteousness is
called the essential (*formalem*) or actual (*activam*) righteousness. Now the thing was thus with me: though I lived
as a holy and blameless monk, I still found myself a great
sinner before God and of a fearful and restless conscience,
nor did I venture to reconcile God with my satisfaction and
merits. For this reason I did not at all love this angry and
righteous God who punishes sinners, but I hated him and (if
this was no blasphemy or to be deemed such) was secretly
angry with God and with real seriousness against him, saying
often: Is it not enough for God that upon us poor, miserable
sinners and by original sin already condemned to death, he lays
all manner of misery and tribulation of this life besides the
terrors and threats of the Law, that by means of the Gospel
he must increase this misery and grief, and by its preaching
and voice further threaten and proclaim his righteousness and
serious wrath? Here I often grew indignant in my puzzled
conscience; yet I continued with beloved Paul in further contemplation, what he may have meant in this place, and had a
hearty thirst and desire to know it. With thoughts of this
kind I spent days and nights, until by the grace of God I
noticed how the words were connected, namely thus: The
righteousness of God is revealed in the Gospel, as it is written:
the just shall live by his faith. By this I learned to understand this righteousness of God in which the righteous by
God's grace and gift alone lives from faith, and noticed that
the apostle's thought was this, that by the Gospel the righteousness which avails before God is revealed, in which God
justifies us from grace and pure mercy by faith, which in
Latin is called *justitiam passivam,* as it is written: the just
shall live by his faith. Here I at once felt, that I was born
anew and had found, like a wide opened door, how to enter
paradise itself; now I also looked at the beloved Holy Scriptures in an entirely different way than before; ran, therefore,
quickly through the entire Bible, as I could recall it, and gathered together also in other words all its expositions, that God's

work is called what he, God himself, works: God's power, by which he himself makes us mighty and strong; God's wisdom, that by which he makes us wise; likewise the rest: God's strength, God's salvation, God's glory, *etc.* Just as then I had hated with all earnestness this little word God's righteousness, so now I began contrariwise to esteem it precious and high as my dearest and most comforting word, and this passage in St. Paul was to me in truth the real portal of paradise."

The contents of our text we may arrange in three words: blood, faith, righteousness. The redemption by Christ Jesus occurred by the shedding of his blood; it becomes our own by faith; it is the highest display of God's righteousness, which is love. Besser.

"Also they teach, that men cannot be justified before God by their own powers, merits, or works; but are justified freely for Christ's sake through faith, *when they believe* that they are received into favor, and their sins forgiven for Christ's sake, who by his death hath satisfied for our sins. This faith doth God *impute* for righteousness before him, Rom. 3 and 4." Augsb. Conf. IV.

"Accordingly, the word *justify* here means to declare righteous and free from sin, and for the sake of Christ's righteousness, which is imputed by God to faith (Phil. 3, 9), to absolve one from their eternal punishment." *F. C.* 572, 17. Compare the classical definition of justification in *F. C.* 501, 4, *etc.*

How St. Paul Preaches Justification by Faith.

He sets forth
  I. *For the whole world of sinners*
 II. *The boundless grace of God,*
III. *Providing the all-sufficient blood of Christ,*
 IV. *That through faith in him*
  V. *He forgives us our sins and declares us just.*

Rom. 3, 20-26.

God's Righteousness: the Open Portal of Paradise.

St. Paul and Luther's experience.
I. *God's grace unlocked it with the blood of Christ.*
II. *God's Gospel bids all sinners enter by faith.*
III. *God's judgment awards to all who do enter eternal pardon and peace.*

The Key to Heaven.

I. *Blood.* II. *Faith.* III. *Righteousness.*

Not a Particle of Difference.

I. *We are all sinners.*
II. *We are all justified by grace.*
III. *We are all able to obtain this justification by faith alone.*

Langsdorff.

There is No Difference.

I. *A crushing word,* for it condemns us all because of our sins.
II. *A comforting word,* for it points us all to the only Savior.
III. *A charming word,* for it urges us all to believe.

Langsdorff.

By Grace Alone.

I. *This is what the law proves.*
II. *This is what Christ gives.*
III. *This is what faith receives.*

Apel.

St. Paul's Grandest Sermon on the Righteousness that Avails before God.

I. *What moved God to establish it?*
   1) This that by the works of the Law no flesh is justified in his sight.
   2) Grace, his undeserved love for the sinful world.

II. *How did God establish it?*
   1) Look at the blood on the mercy-seat of the ark in the tabernacle.
   2) Look at the blood of Christ on the cross.
   3) There God's grace and righteousness clasped hands.
   4) Christ's merits purchased our redemption.

III. *How does God transfer it to us?*
   1) Apart from the Law.
   2) Freely, as a gift.
   3) Through the offer of the Gospel (here preached by his apostle to us all).
   4) By kindling saving faith in our hearts.

Here is the inner sanctuary of St. Paul's teaching, the Holy of Holies of the Gospel. This is the man whose conscience spurns all false comforts; whose heart was led from all false Jewish self-righteousness to the light of the righteousness which God prepared in the Gospel; who bore this light with consuming devotion into the world of Jews and Gentiles. The bells of the Reformation ring out a glorious peal in this text. A second Paul, Luther of Wittenberg, takes up the message — once a monk at Erfurt, groaning beneath the burden of his sins, fasting and castigating his body, without consolation and peace, always receiving a stone for bread in the church of the pope — he discovered the Gospel of St. Paul: *solus Christus, sola gratia, sola fide.* Of all the men that have ever lived, our age needs these two, to carry us away from all the false comforts of shallow morality, superficial self-righteousness, pride of human nature and human works, to lead us to the throne of grace, the blood-stained cross of Christ, the open door of faith in the Gospel.

Righteousness — the One Door of Heaven.

I. *We must be righteous, if we would be saved.*
   1) God is righteous, he hates and must hate sin.
   2) None but the righteous can come to God and enter his presence.
   3) Our conscience feels the necessity of being righteous before God.

II. *No righteousness is possible by efforts of our own.*
   1) In a thousand ways men strive after righteousness.
   2) Many think they have attained it.
   3) They all fail utterly — as Scripture, conscience, and experience prove.

III. *There is only one righteousness that counts with God.*
   1) It counts with him because he has prepared it himself.
   2) He has made Christ the propitiation for our sins, through his blood.
   3) The merits of Christ suffice for the sinner before the judgment bar of God's righteousness.

IV. *God imputes righteousness to all who believe.*
   1) Faith means to give up all righteousness of our own and to cast ourselves wholly upon Christ.
   2) The entire Gospel is intended to awaken such faith.
   3) The moment it is kindled God reckons all Christ's merits as ours and declares us just and righteous in his sight.
   4) This declaration stands as long as faith remains.

V. *The righteousness of faith obtains eternal salvation.*
   1) It cancels all sin and guilt forever.
   2) It makes us God's children and heirs.
   3) Every bar between God and heaven, and us is gone.
   4) When death comes Paradise is ours.

THE MAN OF LOVE.
1 Cor. 13, 1-13.

Gregory Nazianzen, one of the three celebrated Cappadocians of the fourth century, who defended the Nicene faith, and one of the most celebrated orators of the early church, writes of this chapter on love, that here we may read what Paul said of Paul. It is certainly true: only a man in whose heart the Spirit of God had kindled and fanned to a steady blaze the flame of true Christian love could serve him as the apostle did in recording the glories of this love. Paul's description is a Psalm, full of the highest and holiest poetic fervor. Yet there is not one extravagant statement, the whole of it followed the most practical of tendencies: to awaken in the hearts of his Corinthian readers a desire for "the greater gifts," and all these are summed up and combined in this chapter, to which Paul himself has given the heading: "a still more excellent way I show unto you," 1 Cor. 12, 31. All the Bible is full of love; its greatest display is the love of God in Christ Jesus, and the Savior's own love in loving us even unto death. All the saints of God are beautiful in love. Among the apostles one especially has his name linked with love, St. John, the apostle whom Jesus loved, who wrote that God is love, and who enjoined upon us all that we love one another. Peter wrote: "Obeying the truth through the Spirit unto unfeigned love of the brethren, see that ye love one another with a pure heart fervently." 1 Pet. 1, 22. It could not be otherwise: they who had tasted the love of Christ were themselves filled with love; they preached and taught love as the essential fruit of faith, and they were constrained by love in all their life and work. We need this Gospel of love, for ever there is a tendency to forsake the first love (Rev. 2, 4), yea, to lose love altogether by falling again into the love of the world. What a privilege, then, to renew our contact with a man of God whose entire Christian live is a living illustration of the love he so eloquently portrayed for us. It is Paul's heart that lies open before us in this chapter on love; here is the motive power that sent him over land and sea to preach to others the unsearchable riches of Christ; here is the inner power that sustained him amid all his labors, burdens, trials, sufferings, persecutions; here is what made him rise superior to hunger and hardship, false friends and bitter foes, bodily infirmity and dangers of death. Only then will we understand this man when we read the secret of the love of Christ that was poured out in his heart. All his great gifts and abilities, his high and holy office, his exalted position in the church, his stupendous task and astounding success — all of them are what they are and what they came to be, because of his love. To see and feel what Christ's love thus accomplished in this man must stimulate and vivify our lagging love. Away with the dead ashes that cover it, bring on this new fuel, and let the Spirit of love fan our hearts to a holy glow that will never again grow faint and cold.

(13, 1) **If I speak with the tongues of men and of angels, but have not love, I am become sounding brass, or a clanging cymbal.**

When a man with love in his own heart speaks of love he is prone to use a personal touch; so in these opening verses Paul uses the first person: "I." "He passes this judgment by way of example upon himself: that if he were such a one; in order the more to startle others." Luther. Paul uses the vivid form of condition, ἐάν with the subjunctive, but hardly because he expected this condition at some time to be actually fulfilled in himself; the case he states is really only a supposed one, though he presents it in a vivid and realistic form for greater rhetorical effect. — To **speak with the tongues of men** is to use other tongues, languages, or dialects, which the speaker had never learned. So the apostles and others spoke at Pentecost. This was a direct and miraculous gift of the Spirit, and was bestowed frequently in the first church, also at Corinth. The Pentecost miracle is clear evidence that these tongues were understood by hearers who were native to them; of course, where none such were present, the tongues were unintelligible and needed interpretation. These miracles, like healing *etc.*, were signs, and not intended for the ordinary work of preaching and teaching. The Corinthians placed too high an estimate upon this gift, so that the apostle had to correct them. It is for this reason also that he here brings in "tongues," to show how much higher the heavenly gift of love is to be rated. — The addition: **and of angels** outbids what the Corinthians knew in this line. When angels speak to men they use human language, but Daniel, and John in Revelation, and Paul himself when caught up to Paradise heard unutterable things, the tongues of angels as they speak in heaven. Paul puts the thing into the superlative: suppose that I as the apostle of the Lord have the highest possible gift of tongues, those that men use and those even that angels use — how you Corinthians would admire, even envy me, and desire to have an equal gift. — But what about such gifts? Ἀγάπην δὲ μὴ ἔχω, **but** (if I) **have not love** — even these gifts would be all in vain. Here is the theme of the entire chapter: ἀγάπη, "charity," A. V.; far better: **love.** The entire description shows that love to men is meant, and this in its widest range. Ἀγάπη is a much deeper word than φιλία; the love of affection. Wohlenberg says, the word is not unknown in the Greek outside of the Scriptures, but it is really at home only in the Bible. It here points to love as copied after God's love; it always implies that love is directed by reason, spiritual intelligence, and that it is the outcome of a renewed nature, the work of a heart centered in God and his love. In this grand sense it was, of course, impossible for pagan Greek to use the word. — When love is wholly absent, we know that its root is also dead, namely faith. Yet μὴ ἔχω may refer also to occasions and times when a believer speaks (Paul mentions miraculous speaking) or acts in a sinful way, from pride or some other evil motive, and thus "have not love." In both cases: **I am become sounding brass, or a clanging cymbal.** The verb is put forward, γέγονα, I have become, and thus am now, nothing more. But the perfect shows that with all the development and attainment of the past I have now come to nothing more. The man who leaves love out gets nowhere. By χαλκός is meant brass as used in trumpets or other wind instruments; these sound, resound, give a powerful, penetrating tone. It is the same with the cymbal; ἀλαλάζειν is used of the loud battle yell, or of shrieks over the dead. Both the nouns and the appended participles are superlatives as to sound producing power. They offset the superlative idea in "tongues of men and of angels." All such superlative speaking, ranked as the very highest kind of a gift by the Corinthians, would be nothing but an empty tremendous noise — if without love. He who would speak thus, lacking love, would be like dead brass which another makes to sound or ring. The idea that another is the real speaker in the gift of tongues underlies the comparison. Also this, that the gift itself is only an instrument to be used with love, for a higher purpose, not merely for the gratification of pride, or for show. We may apply this thought to the possessors of eloquence in oratory to-day.

(2) **And if I have** *the gift of* **prophecy, and know all mysteries and all knowledge; and if I have all faith, so as to remove mountains, but have not love, I am nothing.**

The repetition of κἂν ἔχω divides the condition into two main parts; the thought again deals with superlatives, but so as to exceed what was said in the first verse. By προφητεία is meant the gift of prophecy, such as the prophets of old had, and others in the New Testament times. This is a higher gift than speaking with tongues; although it is well to remember that God is able to use some very unworthy persons for prophesying: Bileam, King Saul, and Caiaphas (John 11, 51). — But Paul wants the superlative of prophecy, so he adds τὰ μυστήρια πάντα καὶ πᾶσαν τὴν γνῶσιν, for which the appropriate verb εἰδῶ is inserted.

The sentence is cumulative: prophecy, and this so as to include all mysteries, and in addition all knowledge. One might be a prophet and know very few mysteries; and one might know all mysteries and yet lack some other point of knowledge. All three belong to one general class, the mark of which is knowledge, over against mere utterance in the gift of "tongues." What prophet ever knew all the mysteries of God's plans in grace and providence — to say nothing of lesser mysteries? And then the territory outside of mysteries, $\gamma\nu\tilde{\omega}\sigma\iota\varsigma$ in general, and of this the whole of it, $\pi\tilde{\alpha}\sigma\alpha\nu\ \tau\dot{\eta}\nu\ \gamma\nu\tilde{\omega}\sigma\iota\nu$, everything that can be called knowledge. There is little difference whether the article is used as here: "all knowledge," or omitted, as in 1 Cor. 1, 5: "every knowledge." Robertson, 772: "There is an element of freedom in the matter." — To what pertains to the tongue and to the intellect Paul now adds what pertains to the heart: $\pi\tilde{\alpha}\sigma\alpha\nu\ \tau\dot{\eta}\nu\ \pi\iota\sigma\tau\iota\nu$, **all faith,** including everything that can be termed so, but as we at once see by the addition, not "faith" in the sense of saving trust in Jesus Christ, for he who has that has the root of all love, and could never be $o\dot{v}\theta\acute{\epsilon}\nu$. A faith is meant that is able to do miracles, in the sense in which Jesus speaks of it Matth. 7, 22: "Lord, Lord, have we not . . . in thy name cast out devils? and in thy name done many wonderful works?" Here again Paul supposes the superlative degree: "*all* faith," and as a supreme specimen of its work: "so as to remove mountains," $\mu\epsilon\theta\iota\sigma\tau\acute{\alpha}\nu\epsilon\iota\nu$, transfer them to a new location. The expression is proverbial (comp. Matth. 17, 20; 21, 21) and is equal to saying: perform what seem to be not merely impossibilities, but the greatest of impossibilities. — But all this that Paul has piled up — without ἀγάπη, it all not only amounts in itself to nothing, but I, if I have it, I myself οὐθέν εἰμι, I with it all am nothing, οὐδέ + ἕν = not one thing. Men may admire, honor, elevate me, the real inner essential of personal value is gone, its place is a vacuum. Any good I may do with these stupendous gifts is no mark of my own value, and no credit to my own person. The Lord's own verdict is: "I never knew you," Matth. 7, 23. Here indeed there is light on much of the learning, philosophy, science, and great achievements of to-day, outside of Christ, faith, and Christian love.

(3) **And if I bestow all my goods to feed** *the poor,* **and if I give my body to be burned, but have not love, it profiteth me nothing.**

This third comparison rounds out the entire thought. Paul has spoken thus far of gifts (not dwelling on any particular exercise of them); now he adds voluntary deeds of apparent unselfishness, yea, self-sacrifice. The verb ψωμίζω means to feed by giving, bites of food into the mouth, and then in general to divide out to the poor; usually the personal object is mentioned, here it is omitted. Paul again states a superlative case: **all my goods,** all my possessions and property. "To give," writes Luther, "is indeed a fruit of love, yet it is not love itself. Love is a spiritual gift which moves the heart and not only the hands. Love is the name not for what the hand does, but for what the heart feels." The works of love may thus be imitated by those who have no love, yet desire the praise of love. — As a companion piece to this apparent unselfishness Paul places what exceeds it, a superlative exhibition of self-sacrifice: **if I give my body to be burned,** καυχήσωμαι, not, as a few texts read, καυθήσωμαι a fut. sub., which would be a barbarism, to say nothing of the strange sense: "that I may glory," which certainly does not deserve the place given it in the margin of the R. V. The idea usually connected with this burning is that of suffering martyrdom by fire. But cases of this kind did not occur until much later. Meyer thinks Paul may have had in mind Dan. 3, 19 *etc.*, or 2 Macc. 7. B. Weiss refers to tortures of witnesses by means of glowing tin, which Seneca called *ignis*. The word as here used is quite general, although it seems fair to conclude that Paul meant a suffering in behalf of some fellow man, say to shield or protect him. To give or deliver the body to be burned may or may not include the sacrifice of life itself; in either case, however, the self-sacrifice would seem to reach the highest pitch. — And yet all this, without love, **profiteth me nothing,** and the οὐδέν stands forward: not a thing does it profit me. Here again is a step in the gradation: first the gift itself is likened to the sound of brass; next the man who has the gifts is said to be nothing; and now any credit or profit that might come to him from God for his deeds are declared nothing. Jerome: "It is terrible to say, but it is true, if we suffer martyrdom in order to be admired by the brethren, our blood is spilled in vain." "O how many marks of immortal human fame are mortal before God and do not follow their doers, because they have not been made alive by immortal love." Besser. The inside of many a deed looks different from the outside, and God always lifts up the cover, yea, for his eyes there is no cover.

In this first part of Paul's psalm on love he establishes love's supreme *value,* by showing how *nothing avails without it;* the greatest gifts and the grandest deeds with all their greatness and grandness are nothing, make us nothing, and bring us nothing, if love be absent. A deep and solemn refrain runs through the verses in the repetition of: ἀγάπην δὲ μὴ ἔχω, changing never a syllable. Also there is a narrowing down as we proceed: one might easily speak with tongues and yet lack love; less easily might he know all mysteries *etc.* and be without love; and least of all do we expect kind acts and self-sacrifice without at least some love. When it comes to writing full of the richest thought in just about every word, divine inspiration has exceeded by far all that mere human genius can possibly do.

(4) **Love suffereth long, and is kind; love envieth not;** (5) **love vaunteth not itself, is not puffed up, doth not behave itself unseemly, seeketh not its own, is not provoked, taketh not account of evil;** (6) **rejoiceth not in unrighteousness, but rejoiceth in the truth;** (7) **beareth all things, believeth all things, hopeth all things, endureth all things.**

In the first three verses Paul shows that where love is absent nothing can make good the loss. Now he shows us love present, twice beginning with the subject ἡ ἀγάπη. The Greek like the German is able to use the article with abstract nouns, the English can not. What a loss where love is absent, hence what a gain where it is present! And this in every relation of life, even the most trying, painful, and difficult. Thus Paul a second time shows the exceeding *value* of love by describing *its characteristic fea-*

tures. In doing this he personifies love; and Olshausen says he does this because love is never perfectly represented in any one individual Christian. Incidentally, then, this photograph of love is intended for us to hold beside our love, to see whether the two are exactly alike as they should be.

So Paul pictures to us the essence of love to our brethren and fellow men. Love **suffereth long,** $\mu\alpha\kappa\rho o\theta v\mu\epsilon\hat{\iota}$ — and this first stroke of the brush shows us that the portrait is to be of love amid the sins, evils, and trials of a fallen world. Evil influences would spoil love itself from within, or mar it and destroy it by assaults from without. "Longsuffering" is needed in a world bent upon evil and hurtful ways; to keep calm, to be patient, to bear with it all — this is Paul's first precious mark of love. — But paired with this more passive side is a corresponding activity; love does not simply suffer long, without turning to resentment and indignant retribution, it **is kind,** $\chi\rho\eta\sigma\tau\epsilon\acute{v}\epsilon\tau\alpha\iota$, it shows its possessor to be $\chi\rho\eta\sigma\tau\acute{o}s$, useful, pleasant, mild, friendly; the verb implies that love keeps on in acts of kindness and goodness. These two characteristics of love are highly significant; they are a reflex of the love of God and of Christ to a sinful world. So God has been longsuffering and patient, kind and beneficent to us all along — and we have often been wayward, evil, taxing his patience, and deserving of harshness and hardness instead of mild goodness. Note that Paul does not describe some great, wonderful deed or achievement of love; he prefers to show us how the inner heart of love looks placed in a sinful world. Nor does he picture love in ideal surroundings of friendship and affection, where each kisses the other, but in the hard surroundings of a bad world, where negative influences bring out by contrast its great positive power and value.

Now follows a line of negatives, the last of which is rounded out by its opposite. **Love envieth not,** οὐ ζηλοῖ (ζέω, to seethe), it is without selfish zeal, the passion of jealousy. When love sees another prosperous, rich, high, gifted, it is satisfied and rejoices in his advantages. The principle of the world is the exact opposite: everybody would demand for himself just as much as he sees another have. — Love **vaunteth not itself,** οὐ περπερεύεται, it does not boast or magnify its own real or supposed advantages, gifts, possessions or the like. This mark is the other side of the previous one: love is not envious of the gifts of others, nor boastful of its own. — The latter thought Paul extends: **is not puffed up,** οὐ φυσιοῦται (passive), in the pride of its own conceit, looking down upon others. He who boasts always puffs himself up; to brag we need pride, and both show a lack of love. Run down others, raise up self, this is the temptation that always besets us. The humility of true Christian love is the great virtue we need; for he that exalteth himself shall be abased. — **Doth not behave itself unseemly,** οὐ ἀσχημονεῖ, act contrary to the σχῆμα, the fashion, form, or manner that is proper. This draws a wider circle than the scowl and frown of envy, the loud boast of vaunting, and the haughty carriage of pride. All of them hurt and wound others. But there is a tactlessness that in other ways forgets its own proper place and duty, and fails to accord to others their proper dues of respect, honor, or consideration in general. Love keeps the entire bearing within the most considerate lines, ever thoughtful of others, forgetful of self. Paul himself is a fine example; no matter where, among friends or foes, before people or rulers and kings, he always knew how to act as became his station and the position in which he was placed. Besser rightly asks: "Who taught this tentmaker such noble and beautiful manners, such perfect tact in all his bearing, that even the great ones of this world were compelled to respect him?" — Paul lays open another fold in this spotless garment, showing another part of the design woven into it: **seeketh not its own,** τὰ ἑαυτῆς = the things of itself, its own pleasure, profit, honor or anything else. True love is unselfish — how easily said, how hard to attain! It is selfishness that lies at the root of a thousand evils and sins in the world: as between the rich and the poor, capital and labor, nation and nation, man and man. Cure selfishness and you have started a garden of Eden. As when one draws a beautiful face, making one feature after another stand out till the eyes at last light up the whole and give it complete expression, so in this painting of love the inspired artist paints the eyes full of unselfishness, seeking not its own but that which is another's. Yes, that is love : no envy, no boasting, no pride, no unseemliness — because altogether unselfish. — Now we will the better understand the next feature: **is not provoked,** οὐ παροξύνεται (our word "paroxysm"), is not embittered or enraged by abuse, wrong, insult, injury. Love treats others with kindness, consideration, unselfishness, but in turn receives much of the opposite.

Paul's life was full of this experience especially as coming from his brethren in the flesh who ought to have loved him especially. But he did not accuse them, Acts 28, 19; "bless them which persecute you," Rom. 12, 14. — And now one step farther: **taketh no account of evil,** οὐ λογίζεται τὸ κακόν, does not make a reckoning or account of it, charging it against someone. "Thinketh no evil," A. V., overlooks the article; τὸ κακόν is evil that has been done before the action of the verb takes place, not evil which consists of the evil action of the subject itself. This pairs with the preceding characteristic. Love holds no grudge, it forgives and forgets the wrong; it is neither enraged at the moment, nor does it hold vindictiveness afterwards. Chrysostom has well said: "As a spark falls into the sea and does not harm the sea, so wrong may be done to a loving soul and is soon quenched, without disturbing the soul." — And again the circle that has narrowed grows wider: **rejoiceth not in unrighteousness,** ἐπὶ τῇ ἀδικίᾳ, over wrong, whether in him that does it, or in him that suffers it, or in the wrong itself as done or suffered. By ἀδικία is meant the quality that is contrary to the norm of right, δίκη; it is wrong, injustice in form, immorality, unrighteousness. — Instead of this: **but rejoiceth with the truth,** συνχαίρει δὲ τῇ ἀληθείᾳ, not: "in the truth," A. V. Unrighteousness and truth are opposites, and the highest truth is the Gospel itself. To rejoice together with it is to ascribe joy to the truth itself when it wins its way, conquers the darkness and power of falsehood and makes men free from all unrighteousness and wrong. What a blessed thing when truth wins the day in any department of life, especially the saving truth of Christ in the Gospel. The joy of all true Christian love is in the downfall and abolition of wrong, and in the victory and dominion of truth. For truth is always right, and unrighteousness always wrong. Paul spoke to the point when he made these two opposites. Lack of love, itself wrong, has joy in many a wrong.

(7) The four concluding statements are exceptionally beautiful in their simplicity and symmetry: **beareth all things,** that may be inflicted upon it, even though the load seem too *heavy,* as Paul bore the foolish Galatians (Gal. 3, 1); **believeth all things,** refusing to yield to the suspicions of *doubt* and consequent discouragement, as Paul kept his confidence that the fatherly admonitions he sent to the wayward Corinthians would not be in vain; **hopeth all things,** with eyes fixed expectantly above, whence our help cometh, not yielding to *despair* as regards the future, as Paul hoped on for the obdurate Jews and ceased not his prayer and labors — hope knows no pessimism; **endureth all things,** $\hat{v}\pi o\mu \acute{\epsilon}\nu \epsilon \iota$, strong and steadfast in quiet perseverance, the opposite of $\phi \epsilon \acute{v}\gamma \epsilon \iota \nu$, to give up in defeat. Here we see the inner power of love, her head held high, her eyes bright and shining, her hand steady and true, her heart strong with strength from above. O to have more of this love in our own hearts, homes, churches, and lives generally. This love has been called "the greatest thing in the world." It surely deserves the name. Paul did not describe love in its great works, sacrifices, martyrdoms, triumphs; instead he went into the ordinary circumstances of life as we meet them day by day, and showed us the picture of love as

here it must be. We find easy excuses when great things are made the mark for our attainment; Paul has cut them all off. Be a true every-day Christian in the exercise of love — then all great triumphs of love will take care of themselves. He who fails in the ordinary works of love will not even have a chance when the supreme moment for the performance of the extraordinary comes.

(8) **Love never faileth: but whether** *there be* **prophecies, they shall be done away; whether** *there be* **tongues, they shall cease; whether** *there be* **knowledge, it shall be done away.**

In a third way Paul shows the extreme *value* of love; it *endures* when the charismata come to an end, and among the other possessions which endure (faith and hope) love is *the greatest*. Ἡ ἀγάπη οὐδέποτε πίπτει (some texts ἐκπίπτει), it never falls, so as to fall away and disappear; *hoeret nimmer auf.* "Without change of its inner essence love passes over into eternal joy, because it is eternal life already in time." Besser. And as love itself never ceases, so also "its operation, its life and blessing, its beauty and power," Osiander. — Δέ is adversative and prevents us from reading: "Love never faileth, even if prophecies shall be done away," *etc.* Εἴτε δὲ προφητεῖαι is thus a conditional clause with the verb omitted; so the two following clauses — "but whether there be prophecies." By προφητεῖαι are meant the charismatic gifts of prophecy; not the truths or facts prophesied, for these too shall endure. The conditional form itself: "whether there be," points to the temporary character of these gifts; for there are times when these gifts are withheld by the Spirit. But any and all **prophecies** καταργηθήσονται, shall be made useless or void, shall be abolished, and thus shall cease. The gift of prophecy is certainly wonderful, highly to be prized, and precious to the church — think of the prophets of the Old Test., and those of the New. But while they left us what we must all prize and utilize, their gift itself has ceased, and they have had no successors. — It is the same with **tongues,** *i. e.* the gifts of tongues in the early church; παύσονται, they shall stop, and they have stopped already. — So too γνῶσις, **knowledge,** in the sense of a gift, *i. e.* the intellectual ability of handling revealed truth and presenting it in learned form. This, like "prophecies," shall be done away. Paul in these future tenses καταργηθήσονται and παύσονται points to a time when all the precious and notable gifts found in the church shall have completely served their purpose and be done away with for good and all. That will be at the return of Christ, when the kingdom of grace itself shall cease, or rather be completely merged in the kingdom of glory. Then there will be no more prophets, for heaven itself will reveal all its mysteries to us directly; no more tongues and languages, for we shall all understand and speak the language of heaven; no more study, reasoning, learning, for instead of this gift of a few, on which the many depend, the new earth shall be filled with the knowledge of the glory of the Lord, as the waters cover the sea, Hab. 2, 14. But love? — love shall not pass away with these, for love is not a possession that serves only temporary purposes.

(9) For we know in part, and we prophesy in part: (10) but when that which is perfect is come, that which is in part shall be done away.

Here is the reason (γάρ) why two of these gifts shall not and can not endure. Not that there are no other reasons, but this one is all-sufficient for the apostle's purpose. The "tongues" are not mentioned; they stand lowest of the three — though the Corinthians would probably have ranked them on a level with the other two, and most certainly above love. It is quite self-evident that tongues and language as we know them here are not to endure eternally; the penalty of Babel is not to be carried into the other world. As the γλῶσσαι are thus dropped, so already in verse 8 Paul dropped the πίστις he mentioned in verse 2; most likely because he would have had to add a lengthy explanation to differentiate this "faith" from the one he meant to mention at the end. — Ἐκ μέρους is put forward for emphasis; it is the opposite of ἐκ τοῦ παντός. Our knowing is **in part,** partial, and thus inadequate; we do not know with full comprehension, full penetration, complete mastery. In all our knowing there is something left that we do not know, there is always a beyond, to which our little brain and intellectual ability does not reach. It is so also with prophesying. We constantly come to impassable barriers. Speculation tries to leap them, but fails to secure anything but a lot of uncertainties. It is a prime theological and Christian virtue to stop with what the Word of God tells us, and not try to go beyond. This seems humiliating to many, but their efforts to proceed farther only lead them into the bogs and swamps of error. And many of the things the Scriptures do tell us — how inadequately are we able to apprehend them intellectually: the Trinity, the Incarnation, the workings of providence, *etc.* Ever we arrive where Paul did in Rom. 11, 33. It is the same in the domain of nature: what is life, light, electricity, matter, and a thousand things? We do not know what they really are, we know only this or that about them. In the words of a great scientist: *Ignoramus, ignorabimus;* we do not know, nor shall we ever here below know. The foolish pride of scientists is vain. This discounting of knowledge and prophecy is not intended to destroy the value of what we do know; for to know God and Christ in faith is life eternal for us, John 17, 3. But all the forms of our earthly knowing and prophesying of spiritual things shall serve only this earthly and temporal purpose; eventually both shall be superseded. — This shall be **when that which is perfect is come,** ὅταν δὲ ἔλθῃ τὸ τέλειον. We are not to understand, as Hofmann thinks: τὸ τέλειον γινώσκειν καὶ προφητεύειν; the term τὸ τέλειον means much more, it is the perfection of the coming eternal life and of the consummation of salvation. The word has in it the idea of τέλος or goal; that which is perfect is the perfection which will be reached when we all arrive at the eternal goal set us by Christ. Τὸ τέλειον will be attained when Christ returns at the last day, when his kingdom is fully come, when we are glorified with him in heaven. Then all this piece business of earth will be abolished; it will have served its purpose; an entirely new way of apprehending, seeing, and knowing shall take its place. In a way our earthly knowing is perfect, because sufficient for its purpose, enabling us to be saved; but after that in the perfect world something higher and sufficient for that higher life shall be ours. Not that then we shall know all things, omniscience belongs to God alone, even the angels do not know the deep things of God which only the Spirit of God searcheth. But in heaven we shall know in a heavenly manner. Besser says that Melanchthon increased his love of dying by thinking of the joy of knowing the mysteries of the holy Trinity no more merely "in part," but in this heavenly manner.

(11) **When I was a child, I spake as a child, I felt as a child, I thought as a child: now that I am become a man, I have put away childish things.**

A simple and beautiful illustration, in form an analogy; note the oratorical form. But λαλεῖν is not meant to parallel γλωσσολαλεῖν; nor λογίζεσθαι, γινώσκειν; for φρονεῖν in no way matches up with the third member left, namely with προφητεύειν. Paul merely compares his childhood with our present state in this life, and his manhood, so different from everything childish, and such an advance upon it, with our future state in glory. Even so, the analogy is only partly illustrative; though this point holds, that the child is in the man fully developed, and so we who are now in lowliness will be the ones eventually glorified. The full flower bursts or sheds the rough petals which protected the bud. **I felt** as a child, ἐφρόνουν, points to the thoughts, interests, and strivings of a child; ἐλογιζόμην, **I thought** = I judged. The two perfect tenses γέγονα and κατήργηκα refer to the past as their effect continues in the present: I have become, and thus I now am and continue to be; I have put away, and I am now as one that has done this.

(12) **For now we see in a mirror, darkly; but then face to face: now I know in part; but then shall I know even as also I have been known.**

Paul might have kept on throughout with the singular, using himself to individualize and make concrete the truth he was expounding. It is a masterly touch to insert this one **we** among the "I" sentences; it shows clearly that what he says refers to all his readers. The verb βλέπομεν has and needs no object here, for it is the quality and act of the seeing itself (no matter what the spiritual object) that is meant. An ἔσοπτρον is a **mirror,** not as some have thought, colored and ornamental glass as used in church windows. Wohlenberg assures us that windows of this kind were known in the days of the emperors, and were termed *specularia,* but the term for such a window is δίοπτρον or δίοπτρα; hence also any reference to Num. 12, 8 is shut out. Rabbinical tradition may have figured out that Moses saw God through a window of single glass, the prophets through one with nine thicknesses of glass; any notion of this kind is surely excluded here in Paul's words. Only we will have to remember that the ancients knew no mirrors of glass as we do, their ἔσοπτρα being made of polished metal which reflected an image faintly, without sharp and distinct outlines. The point of the illustrative (γάρ) statement, then, is this: we do not see divine things directly, we catch only the more or less indistinct reflections of them as the mirror of God's Word shows them to us. The fact is that God himself had to condescend to us in the Word and speak of heavenly things in a human way, because only in this way could he at all impart them to us. To speak in a heavenly way would have defeated his saving purpose; and to show us heavenly things directly, without the mirror of his Word, would simply have blinded and destroyed us. Thus the Word is indeed clear, and all its statements shining truth; but nothing to what we shall see and have when we see "face to face" above. — It is best to take ἐν αἰνίγματι as further defining the manner of βλέπομεν ἄρτι, hence omitting a comma in front of it. **Darkly** really means: in an enigma; in a riddle. What is meant is very plain, when we recall how the Scriptures constantly use earthly and human terms for divine and supernatural things. Think of the parables, the types, the thousands of figures and comparisons, Paul using human illustrations right here. Every such term and expression is really a riddle, and we know what foolish solutions many readers have given them. The LXX in Num. 12, 8 has οὐ δι' αἰνιγμάτων, and it is possible that Paul's similar phrase is an allusion (which is very far from a quotation). — But all this shall cease when we enter this heavenly state (τότε); **then face to face,** πρόσωπον πρὸς πρόσωπον, the former a nominative in apposition to the subject of βλέπομεν, the latter referring to the object which at first was not mentioned, which is God, as the following statement shows. Yonder we will need no medium, not even the divine Word. We shall see Jesus as he is, 1 John, 3 2; yea, even God himself, Matth. 5, 8; now we can see both only in the Word and as their works in nature and grace reflect them. This direct seeing will be our eternal joy and blessedness. — Paul repeats: **now I know in part,** again with concrete personal individualization, in order to place over against this the glorious heavenly opposite: **but then,** *etc.* For the words ἐπιγνώσομαι καθὼς καὶ ἐπεγνώσθην the American Committee proposes: "then I shall know fully even as also I have been known fully," differentiating the compound verb from the simple form. Both verbs here are taken by commentators in the intensified sense: the knowing of loving appropriation. The aorist ἐπεγνώσθην refers to an act of knowing which precedes the time of the future tense in the first verb. Most commentators refer this aorist to the time of Paul's election or conversion, and Meyer exclaims as regards the latter: "For the apostle himself, what a great memory!" The thought, then, is not that we shall know as God knows in general, for even in heaven our knowledge cannot compare with God's as to comprehensiveness; but as God with direct loving knowledge embraced every one of his children, when he chose them in eternity or when they became his by faith, so we at last shall in love know God by direct contact. Think how far this leaves behind all the mediated knowing that is possible to us now! Wohlenberg would not restrict the aorist to Paul's election or conversion, but prefers to put into it all God's embrace of loving knowledge directed towards his children; the tense will bear also this interpretation.

(13) **But now abideth faith, hope, love, these three; and the greatest of these is love.**

Some take νυνί temporal, as referring to our earthly life, making faith, hope, and love endure for this life, and love the greatest of these for this period.

They usually interpret, however, that faith and hope will end with this life, faith giving place to sight, and hope attaining its object and thus ceasing to be hope; while, they say, love will go on forever, thus proving it is greatest. But Paul does not in this way exalt love over the other two. He has hitherto spoken of the gifts that shall be done away with and cease altogether when we attain heaven; among them he has not listed faith and hope. He has implied however, that love shall not end as to the gifts he has mentioned. Love indeed manifests itself imperfectly here, and God will perfect it too at last; but Paul does not speak of this, he implies only that love shall undergo no change like knowledge, and suffer no abolition and general transformation as knowledge must. Here now he turns from the things that must fall away, to those that shall abide, μένει, and he has already said that love οὐδέποτε πίπτει. Is love the only possession we have which lasts like this? Paul says there are three of this kind: **faith, hope, love.** In a certain way it is true indeed, faith shall turn to sight, 2 Cor. 5, 7, inasmuch as the Word, the medium for faith now, will be taken away and we shall see Christ as he is. But in another way it is true that **faith** shall abide eternally, namely our trust in God and our Savior and the Holy Spirit, for to all eternity our salvation will rest on them, and ever it will be our faith which connects us with them. This is what Paul means with μένει πίστις. So νυνὶ δέ is not temporal, but logical: **but now** with things so as just stated (in 8-12). And we must keep to what Paul says here, where he plainly gathers the greatest things together which all pass away, but does not list among them faith; nor is the contrast he has in mind between faith and sight, but between faith as that which connects us eternally with God and the greatest of God's other gifts in the church which though great pass away. — So also **hope.** The thought is not as in Rom. 8, 24 *etc.*, where hope, a sure expectation, based on solid grounds, is set over against its consummation, the final actual possession and enjoyment of what we hoped for. Here, as Meyer says, hope refers to the eternal duration and development of the glory in heaven. And Kling writes, that hope is to remain as the expectation of an ever new and higher unfolding of glory in the future state. Hope in heaven is the certainty of the glorified soul directed towards the things that lie before it in the state of perfection. It is not correct to think that when once we reach heaven there will be nothing more for us to look forward to. The angels sing ever new praises to God; so shall we as we pass to one after another of the things that God has prepared for us above. It is difficult to speak of this subject, for in reality eternity is not time, not even an endless time. Human thought is fettered to time conceptions even when thinking of eternity. So we can speak of hope in heaven only in this human way. But the glories of God are exhaustless, and in heaven we shall never get through exploring them. And thus we shall go on in hope: μένει ἐλπίς. — Paul uses one μένει for all three: faith, hope, **love.** The sentence is built so, that if faith and hope remain only until we enter heaven, love too would remain only that long. It is impossible to drop faith and hope at the golden portal, and take love in with us. This is prevented in still another way, namely when Paul adds with great emphasis: τὰ τρία ταῦτα, tying a band about these three, as if, after naming them, he asked us to stop a moment and contemplate these three, which constitute one class of spiritual possessions, one enduring eternally, over against the other class, those that endure only for time. — But even so, love has the preeminence; not indeed as *outlasting* the other two, for all three last alike to all eternity, but as *outranking* the other two. Of the three love is queen: μείζων δὲ τούτων ἡ ἀγάπη. Paul does not say in what respect love is greater, μείζων, than faith and hope, but all commentators try to answer the question. The best answer is the one which recalls that God himself is love. Bengel: *"Ac Deus non dicitur fides aut spes absolute, amor dicitur."* It is love that makes us like God. "For love is of God; and every one that loveth is born of God, and knoweth God." 1 John 4, 7. Also verse 12: "If we love one another, God dwelleth in us, and his love is perfected in us." And especially verse 16: "God is love; and he that dwelleth in love dwelleth in God, and God in him." What John here says of our love while in this earthly state may surely be used to cast a light upon our state above, where it will be love that brings us into the full union and communion of God. Faith's nature is to receive, but love gives; and giving is greater than receiving. God's fullest purpose is attained in us when we are filled with love. So hope also looks forward to receiving, but love is full possession and completed joy. And for every new joy hope receives in heaven love will be the response on our part. It will be love by which we rest on the bosom of God.

HOMILETICAL HINTS.

Paul's description of love is the epistle text for Quinquagesima. In spite of this we have placed the text in this brief series, for in any line of texts aiming to set before us St. Paul as he really was, and as the church must ever know him, this text on "charity" or love is quite indispensable. Not only is the text rich enough to stand repeated preaching on it, in our series it will also receive a treatment different from the one naturally accorded it in the Sunday morning series for the church year. There it helps to usher in Lent, and its doctrinal contents as they stand alone will occupy the preacher; here St. Paul himself is our theme, and the sermon will connect all that he writes of love with his person, character, and life. A man of mighty charismatic gifts was he, yet he valued all these gifts only as they deserved; he knew the supreme value of those possessions which the Gospel bestows, not only upon a few chosen individuals, but upon all true followers of Christ, the value of faith, hope, and love, and especially also the surpassing value of the latter. This is the man who by the Spirit speaks to us here. We shall know the better what he tells us for knowing him himself. — Like the foregoing this text is great and rich enough to have several sermons preached on it; our brief series on St. Paul may thus be lengthened if desired.

The translation "charity" is peculiarly unhappy. Neither in its primary signification, nor in the sense which usage has attached to it, does it properly express what Paul wrote. Many a man has been led to think that almsgiving covers a multitude of sins, because charity is said to have that effect, according to the faulty translation of 1 Pet. 4, 8. Likewise that kindness to the poor and the sick is the sum of all religion, because Paul is conceived as exalting charity above faith and hope. Here the preacher has a duty to perform.

Paul's picture of love is ideal, and yet he was writing with the practical object of filling the hearts of his Christian Corinthians with this very love. To a very great extent Paul realized in his own life what here he portrayed for the Corinthians and us all. Among the preachers who have taken up this text from the practical side, putting Paul himself into this chapter, Louis Harms stands as one of the best. We appropriate a number of his thoughts.

God does not demand of us great skill and ability, only love. When this is fervent and heartfelt, without guile, God is pleased, and this delights and rejoices him more, and he has his pleasure in it far beyond, all the art and wisdom of men. J. Arndt.

"As every lovely hue is light,
So every grace is love."

"Love feels no burdens, regards no labors, would willingly do more than it is able, pleads not impossibilities, because it feels sure that it can and may do all things. Love is swift, sincere, pious, pleasant, and delightful; strong, patient, faithful, prudent, longsuffering, manly, and never seeking itself; it is circumspect, humble, upright; sober, chaste, steadfast, quiet, and guarded in all its senses." Thomas à Kempis.

"Love is the ligament which binds together the several members of the body of Christ, the cement which keeps the stones of the temple together. Without love there can be no body, no temple, only isolated stones or disconnected, and therefore useless, members." *Exp. of the B.* Bunyan says: "Is it so much to be a fiddle?"

To pay ten, twenty dollars and more for a fine dress, coat, or cloak, or for gold and silver chains and ornaments, that is a trifle. To put through ten, twenty dollars, or to gamble them away in a night, is a joke. But to offer one dollar for the poor, or for the conversion of the heathen, or for other works of love and mercy, that is too much, and we exclaim: We cannot stand it! Harms.

What planted, founded, and spread Christianity over the whole world? What now moves men to conversion from darkness to light and from the power of Satan to God? Is it not the power of preaching, human speech? And yet without love this advantage of human speech is nothing but loss, yea double damnation. Yea, you may be assured that if the apostle Paul, who by the power of his preaching turned many to Christ, had not been able to say: "The love of Christ constraineth me," he would have accomplished nothing with his eloquence. Take a preacher, who speaks ever so touchingly and beautifully of Christian love, and urges this love upon every one, and proves to them, that real faith is the faith that is active in love; but this same preacher is a tyrant at home toward his wife and children, or in his conversation among his members, serves the devil of selfishness with usury, avarice, and haughty, hard language — do you think that he will have fruit? I tell you he will not; every one will turn in disgust from him and call him a hypocrite. Harms.

He also speaks of Paul's collection for the famine sufferers (2 Cor. 8-9): "But if Paul and the Christians had laid their hands in their laps, and had done nothing for the poor to relieve them in the famine, what would their prophesying have amounted to? It was the love with which Paul and his assistants collected rich gifts for the poor Christians and brought these gifts to the suffering congregation at Jerusalem, that made their prophesying a blessing. . . . I know no apostle, and in fact no man, who had such an extraordinary measure of divine knowledge, such experience in divine mysteries, as the apostle Paul. Read diligently in his Epistles and you will find this. So clearly, so plainly, so exactly and definitely as he does, no other apostle expresses himself in regard to the most mysterious doctrines of Christianity. But what good would this have been if Paul with all his knowledge and insight had sat behind the stove and kept his pound in the napkin — would not his knowledge have turned out to his own injury and damnation? for let no one put his light under a bushel! But Paul used his gift; his love to Christ and his love to his poor fellow men drove him out and constrained him to travel without rest in the world, as far as his feet could carry him, to preach and teach everywhere, yea, when he lay a prisoner to write with a chain on his wrists. And it was this glowing love of the apostle that made his knowledge and experience a blessing; and thousands and thousands praise him as the rescuer of their souls.

Did not Peter walk on the sea? by faith heal the sick and raise the dead? But imagine for a moment, when in Joppa faithful Dorcas had died, and the Christians in Joppa sent for Peter who was in Lydda, that he should hurry and come to them, and Peter had had no love in his heart, and had remained with his faith in Lydda in order to have a pleasant time, would not his faith have turned out for his own injury and damnation?

The great building of evangelical doctrine has many a gap which demands that we wall it up; but these gaps are windows, from which we may look up to heaven, in expectation of the coming of that which is perfect. Besser.

Like a diligent little bee Paul has carried together all the parts that belong to love and joined them into one; so that we can call it Paul's golden chain of Christian love, its nature and attributes, and this with fifteen links and a clasp or catch by which to fasten them on. V. Herberger.

We know a good deal about Paul's intercourse with others, and many of the trying situations in which he was placed. His love everywhere shines out with singular beauty. Read for example Acts 20. His prayer, his tears, his anxieties, his labors, all were filled with love. Nor was his love flabby, flattering, loose and liberalistic, merely trying to please men; we know how he resisted Peter when this apostle erred in his actions at Antioch, and how he warned and rebuked his congregations. It was the strong love of a strong man, with a mighty faith in his soul.

In heaven love will be our law, the Son our King, and to praise and magnify God our greatest work. Bernhard of Clairvaux.

An old proverb: Friends in need go 100 to the ounce, and if they are to aid us, 100 to the grain.

It is the imperfect knowledge of the child which leads it on to further attainment. The fundamental doctrine of the Christian creed that there are three Persons in one God is certainly a very rough and childish expression of a truth far deeper than we can understand, but to reject this doctrine because it is evidently only an approximation to a truth which cannot be defined and stated in final terms is to refuse to submit to the conditions under which we now live and to ape a manhood which in point of fact we do not possess. *Exp. of the B.*

Among the obvious divisions of the matter contained in this text are the following: Harms: True Christian love — 1) Its value; 2) Its nature; 3) Its duration. — Reim: The Glory of Love — 1) It exceeds everything; 2) It conquers everything; 3) It outlasts everything. — M. Frommel: The New Testament Canticles of Love — 1) Love ennobles all gifts; 2) Consecrates all fellowship; 3) Outlasts all things temporal. — Paul's Praise of Christian Love — 1) Its depth; 2) Its breadth; 3) Its length; 4) Its height. — Harms works in abundant material from Paul's life, but most of the sermon writers fail to do this.

St. Paul: A Life under the Dominion of True Christian Love.

I. *All his gifts were consecrated by it.*
1) He speaks hypothetically here, but think of the gifts he really had.
2) Love put them all into the highest possible service, with the most wonderful devotion.
3) The results as we see them in his labors, as we enjoy them in his inspired writings.
4) God's estimate of such a life.

II. *All his actions are ennobled by it.*
1) Not merely in the great, but also in the little things of life. He thinks of what the Corinthians lacked and should and could have, letting them look at the motives he fostered in his own heart.
2) He showed them how he would have his heart and acts: when he himself prospered; when he himself lacked or suffered; when others prospered; when others suffered; when others ill-treated him; when others went astray.
3) The mighty encouragement an example like Paul's must be to us all.

III. *All his future was made glorious by it.*
   1) The things he expected to outgrow and leave behind like a child coming to manhood.
   2) The permanent things that he would take with him (faith, hope, love).
   3) The crowning possession, love in the presence of divine love above.

The Great Doctrine of St. Paul: Love is the True Measure of a Man.

It measures
   I. *Even his greatest gifts and achievements.*
      1) How Paul measured his.
      2) How he reckoned their value.
   II. *As well the smallest detail of daily conduct.*
      1) A glance at these details, as Paul met them daily.
      2) A man's measure when in these things he lacks love.
      3) A man's measure when in these things, like Paul, he has and exercises love.
   III. *Finally also the eternal sum of his life.*
      1) Paul knew what would fall away when God measured his life at last;
      2) Also the possessions that count without fail in that final measuring;
      3) And the one that then counts as the crown of all.

Did men appreciate St. Paul when he labored for them and among them? We know that many did not. Nor did they appreciate Christ when he was among men.

Paul, an Example of the Hidden Worth of Love.

   I. *The apostle's apparent greatness.*
   II. *The apostle's true greatness.*
   III. *The eyes which alone are able to distinguish the two.*

---

1 Cor. 13, 1-13.

The Excellency of Christian Love.

I. *It is a state of grace.*
II. *It is a fountain of blessings.*
III. *It is of eternal duration.*

Loy.

A MINISTER OF MINISTERS.
1 Tim. 3, 1-7.

Paul himself was a minister. In Eph. 3, 7 he writes that he was made a minister, διάκονος; he repeats it Col. 1, 23: "the hope of the Gospel which ye heard . . . whereof I Paul was made a minister, διάκονος." What he means by this designation we see in Eph. 4, 11-12, where he names the different kinds of ministrants in the work of the Gospel, all given of God "unto the work of ministering, εἰς ἔργον διακονίας." In Acts 6, 4 we see that the apostles considered their supreme duty ἡ διακονία τοῦ λόγου, "the ministry of the Word. Paul speaks of it in many ways, always glorying in this his high and holy office. Διακονία refers to labor, work, ministration and benefit rendered in accordance with Christ's call and appointment to the church of God; comp. for instance Acts 20, 24. In this ministry the apostle recognized his many associates and fellow ministers, Eph. 6, 21; Col. 1, 7; 4, 7; 1 Tim. 3, 2; *etc*. Though greater as an apostle than the great host of these other ministers Paul loved to range himself alongside of them, delighting in their joint service to others. The apostle has the same position and work in mind when he calls himself "a *servant* of Jesus Christ, called to be an apostle, separated unto the Gospel of God," δοῦλος; comp. Gal. 1, 10: "if I were still pleasing men, I should not be a δοῦλος of Christ." The genitive usually attached shows that servant, bondservant, or slave points to the apostle's

relation to his divine Master. The work he does is
for this Master, although done for men, and he is ever
entirely subservient and obedient to this Master's will
and word alone. — But it was given to this great
διάκονος and δοῦλος Paul, as to none of his fellow apostles, to be a minister not merely of the church in general, but also in a special way a ministrant, servant,
and helper of the ministry itself. We have three letters
of Paul directed to ministers, and in his other letters
he deals variously with the office and work of these
men. It is Paul who has laid down in two places a
summary of the requirements that must be made of
every minister of the church, and besides these basic
statements there is a full discussion on many points
of how a minister ought to behave himself in the house
of God, which is the church of God. 1 Tim. 3, 15. All
this is exceedingly valuable for all time. To know
Paul we ought to know how he looked upon his office
as a minister of the church. As regards his own person there were, of course, special requirements, gifts,
authority, *etc.*, for Paul was an apostle of the Lord.
He emphasizes these things where necessary; in general, however, he delights in the office and work as
he shared it with many men, among them Timothy
and Titus to whom he wrote his pastoral letters. His
desire and effort was to fill the church with good
ministers of Jesus Christ, 1 Tim. 4, 6. And among
all these his fellow ministers he looms up in the full
sense of the word καλὸς διάκονος Χριστοῦ Ἰησοῦ. With
these thoughts in mind we turn to the precious words
with which this good minister served all his fellow
ministers and the church in general, showing them
what a minister of Christ's church must be.

(3, 1) **Faithful is the saying, If a man seeketh the office of a bishop, he desireth a good work.**

Paul has given Timothy, whom he had left in charge at Ephesus to direct the church in general, detailed directions concerning the public worship, how the congregation should pray, how the men, and how the women were to act. It is entirely natural that he should continue to say what was necessary concerning the officers in a congregation, namely the pastor, and then the deacons or helpers. The directions are general, Paul is not referring to Timothy personally, although what is said has its application also to him. The form of expression, laying down in advance what is necessary for a deacon, seems to imply that Timothy on his part see to it that wherever pastors are chosen these essential requirements be observed, also that if any man on his part desire this office he come up to these specifications. It is not necessary at all that Timothy should act the bishop (in the later sense of the word) in executing the apostle's directions; all pastors everywhere are obligated by the apostle's words to do what naturally falls to them in directing their own and other congregations so that only worthy and fitting men may be associated with them in the holy office and be placed in charge of congregations. Timothy held a prominent and very important position as the pastor in Ephesus, having been personally associated with the apostle in his missionary travels and labors, and now with grave responsibilities resting upon him and many looking to him for advice and direction, it was proper and right and a great help to him personally and a blessing to the church as such that Paul should add to his previous instruction these written repetitions and elucidations. — Πιστὸς ὁ λόγος marks the beginning of a new section and at once lays great weight upon what is about to be said. In 1, 15 as here the formula is used to usher in an important statement; in other instances Paul uses it as a seal upon what he has just said. The margin tells us that some would here draw the words to the preceding statement; but is easy to see that they would not fit these nearly as well as they do what follows. On altogether insufficient authority Wohlenberg would read: ἀνθρώπινος ὁ λόγος, instead of πιστός, and translates: "Generally human is the saying." He loses both the proper textual authority and the clearness of Paul's thought. To say that if a man seeks the office of a bishop he desires a *good* work, this Paul writes is a word that is πιστός, reliable and trustworthy indeed. One can depend on it, he is seeking an excellent work, for the office is that in the fullest sense of the word. — Εἴ τις ὀρέγεται, **if a man seeketh,** that is reacheth out or striveth to obtain this office, of course, in a proper Christian manner, with the right motives behind his efforts, to serve Christ and the church, not to lord it over Christ's heritage. When we read the words we may keep in mind that in those early days there was often personal danger connected with the office, and frequently little or no remuneration. To desire the ministry in the right way is always a praiseworthy thing; and it is an honor for any congregation to have furnished a goodly number of men for the holy office. Think of Hermannsburg which has scores of ministers and missionaries in many parts of the world. In too many of our congregations no young man ever aspires to the holy office; this means that the spiritual life in such a congregation is below par and not strong enough to produce this choicest and richest of fruit. — **The office of a bishop** = ἐπισκοπή, etymologically: an overseership. But the word occurs only twice in the New Test. (Acts 1, 20), and infrequently in the LXX. However, its meaning here is altogether assured: the office of supervising, leading and directing the Christian congregation; in other words what we call the office of a minister of the Gospel, or of a pastor. The apostles were the first leaders of the churches which they succeeded in establishing; but when they proceeded to new fields of labor in pursuance of their call to evangelize the world, they arranged for others, capable and reliable, to take over this work. How this was done we see in Acts 14, 23; the congregations chose and thus called their bishops or pastors. These were also called πρεσβύτεροι, elders, a term which refers more to the dignity connected with the office than the other, which refers to the work itself. It may have been that originally the term "bishop" was used by Gentile Christians, while "elder" was used by Jewish Christians, which also would agree with the pre-Christian use of the terms. That the two were used of the same office and the same persons is shown by Acts 20, 17 and 28; Tit. 1, 5 and 7; 1 Pet. 5, 1 *etc*. At first the term "elder" expressed the greater dignity, but afterwards the title "bishop" was used for one who had the oversight of a number of congregations and their pastors; but we must remember that the original office of "elder" and "bishop" is by *divine* arrangement and right, while the later office of "bishop" has only *human* authority behind it. — **He desireth a good work,** not a sinecure, but an ἔργον, for the ministry is indeed labor; compare οἱ κοπιῶντες ἐν λόγῳ καὶ διδασκαλίᾳ, 1 Tim. 5, 17. Bengel: *"Negotium, non otium."* Stellhorn notes, that there is no man living who has more to do than a conscientious preacher; and that the preacher who has nothing to do is a pitiable creature; he has missed his calling. But this labor is not merely as such arduous and taxing to a man's strength, it is at the same tame καλόν, good, excellent, praiseworthy. Καλόν ἔργον ἐπιθυμεῖ — the first word has the accent; and this excellence is easy to perceive: the ministry is a working together with God as no other office or calling can claim to be; a working with the divine Word and sacraments, than which no higher means or instruments exist; a working for man's highest interests, the spiritual and moral, and thus the eternal, besides which all others take second rank. But with this office of so high a character its incumbent must correspond in general character and qualifications. Only excellent men match an excellent office, and this is one supremely excellent.

(2) **The bishop therefore must be without reproach, the husband of one wife, temperate, soberminded, orderly, given to hospitality, apt to teach.**

Δεῖ denotes necessity; all kinds of necessity, and so also the one that fits this case, namely a moral and spiritual necessity. By noting what follows in Paul's specifications we see that he really names nothing but elementary and thus essential requirements; they who would fail to come up to them ought not to be allowed to enter the ministry, and Timothy no doubt understood Paul to mean nothing less. The οὖν connects the necessity involved with the statement that the ministry is "a good work." A good work requires a good worker. This is true at the time when he aspires to the work, but it remains true also for the entire time during which he performs this work. To deviate from the lines here laid down would render a minister of the Gospel unfit for his high calling; his fellow ministers and the church would have to adjudge him as no longer fit, and thus proceed to take the office from him. — The word **bishop,** ἐπίσκοπος, "overseer" (the incumbent of the ἐπισκοπή) occurs but four times in the New Testament. It certainly fits its place well here where the apostle intends to say what kind of a man one must be to be placed over others, to watch over them and direct and lead them, in the very highest concerns of life. The Lord makes requirements of any Christian, he will be doubly particular with Christian overseers, leaders, pastors. — When now we examine the requirements which Paul would have Timothy insist upon, we are struck with the fact that, outside of two of these requirements, they are altogether such as must be made of members of the church generally. The sum of the matter thus is that a pastor must himself be an honorable Christian man, known and acknowledged as such. In addition he must be a teacher and have sufficient experience and balance to do his ministerial work. No requirements are made which would make of the minister a superior order. Only one is our Master, and we all, clergy and laity, are brethren. Nor are there two standards of morality, a higher one for the overseers, and a lower one for those whom they oversee. Any such distinction is vicious and must be rejected. Sometimes church bodies forbid certain things to pastors, such as membership in secret orders, while they refuse to forbid the same things to the members of the church generally; they ought to learn of Paul and Timothy. The pastor is one with his flock, only he is to show the others the way, he is to be their "example," Phil. 3, 17 (Paul himself, an apostle); 2 Thess. 3, 9; 1 Pet. 5, 1-3. They are to walk the same spiritual and moral road, towards the same goal of salvation. Paul teaches no false spirituality for any one, not even for pastors.

The first five requirements thus laid down deal with the bishop's own personal life. He must be **without reproach,** ἀνεπίλημπτον, "blameless" (A. V.), so that no one can rightly take up and prefer a charge against him. This requirement is quite general, and commentators frequently pass over it as though this only sums up what follows. But the text reads as if this requirement is simply coordinated with the following ones. Any man against whom a moral charge of any kind can be substantiated is disqualified for the ministry, no matter what his talents or other qualifications may be. Paul could not have left out ἀνεπίλημπτος, even with all that he here adds, as Tit. 1, 7 shows, where the following specifications do not include everything mentioned in our text. Blamelessness must be required in one way or another, no matter what other qualities are especially named or omitted. And this for a man's entire ministry, so that this term contained an admonition to Timothy himself: he as every minister must not only at first be, but must also remain, blameless. Blamelessness, however, is not sinlessness, nor a perfection that is never guilty of a fault; this would debar us all. Nor is it required of us that no man ever try to blame or charge us with wicked conduct; for efforts in this direction are often made, and many good men have had to suffer, sometimes severely. "Woe unto you, when all men speak well of you! for so did their fathers to the false prophets." Luke 6, 26. Paul has himself defined what he means: "Giving no offense in any thing, that the ministry be not blamed." 2 Cor. 6, 3; Rom. 14, 13. A man who is living and acting offensively, causing others to stumble, is not one adapted to the ministry; and if one already in the ministry do this, he would thereby lose his fitness. When the Gospel arouses opposition and men turn against a minister with hateful accusations, he suffers only what Paul himself suffered, also Timothy whom Paul urged to endure hardness as a good soldier of Jesus Christ. The thing that Paul refuses to condone in a minister is offense on the minister's part, for this would be a reproach to the Gospel and the church, and while bad enough and injurious in any member of the church, much more so in a member who would direct and supervise others.

The husband of one wife, μιᾶς γυναικὸς ἄνδρα. This is a hard text for the celibates of Rome, who sometimes interpret "wife" of the church, saying that they as priests are betrothed to the church. Very inconveniently Paul adds a further statement regarding the bishop's children. The word "one" is a numeral, set over against two or more. But the argument is fallacious that because a bishop was restricted to one, others might belong to the church as members though joined to two or more. This proves too much, for it would follow that while bishops dared not be brawlers, strikers, drunkards, *etc.*, others under certain circumstances might. Nor does Paul here command that every minister be married and shut out unmarried men. Moreover, "one" cannot be absolute so as to deny to pastors the right to marry a second time. This matter is settled by Rom. 7, 1-3; 1 Cor. 7, 8 *etc.* and 39; 1 Tim. 5, 9 *etc.*, where second marriages are placed on a level with first marriages. What the apostle requires is sexual purity, and he speaks of marriage as the rule for pastors. In Ephesus and the Gentile world generally sexual vices of all kinds were the rule; over against these the apostolic convention had laid down a general rule for the entire church, Acts 15, 20 and 29. Paul here repeats this and applies it to aspirants for the ministry. Each pastor was to have his own wife, if he wished, and was to live with her in chastity and honor, avoiding every occasion for slander. Even to-day Paul's word is necessary, for some have stained their lives with sins against the sixth commandment, disgracing their Christian profession and holy calling and causing great offense. — A third personal requirement is added: **temperate.** By νηφάλιον all forms of excess are excluded, for instance in the use of wine or strong drink, as verse 8: μὴ οἴνῳ πολλῷ προσέχοντας. The word is frequently used in its derived meaning: temperate, balanced, restrained in judgment; but when Meyer would restrict it to this, he has insufficient grounds. The temperateness here required will control the minister in all his acts and words, his eating and drinking, his work and pleasure, his expression of opinions and his words generally; in none of these things are his passions to run away with his better judgment. To be "sober" is a general Christian requirement, 1 Thess. 5, 6 and 8; 1 Pet. 1, 13; *etc.;* it certainly applies with special force to the ministry. — Σώφρονα, **soberminded,** is to use sound sense, to be and to act sensibly, with proper self-control. The man who is σώφρων will keep in proper bounds, will avoid excess, even in the use of things right and permissible. The A. V. has "vigilant, sober" for this and the previous virtue; to reverse the two would be nearer what Paul wrote. Temperateness and sensibleness really go hand in hand, and are surely very necessary for one who is set to help others keep in proper bounds. — Paul adds **orderly,** κόσμιον, respectable, "in his walk, his bearing, his gestures, his dress," Wohlenberg. The word is from κόσμος, *mundus,* the world in its orderly arrangement, and κοσμέω, to adorn, arrange, put in order. The entire conduct and life of a pastor ought to be marked by good order, in the sense of good manners. This requirement goes together with the preceding two marks of a Christian pastor; orderliness *est extra* as Bengel writes, but σώφρων is hardly a complete opposite to it and altogether *intus,* as he makes it, for all three have to do with outward conduct, and all three, also κόσμιος, go back to the mind and heart which control our outward life.

The following two characteristics may be combined: **given to hospitality, apt to teach,** since the pastor by virtue of his position in the church was naturally called upon more than others in those early days to entertain strangers. Among them would be other ministers, who would seek out their associates in the office. Persecutions began early and only too frequently assailed the men at the head of the congregations. Many a Christian found that he was no longer welcome among the Gentile relatives and friends who had lodged him before. Besides this, travelers in those days often found little or no accommodations as these may be had now in all our cities and even smaller places. Compare 3 John 5-8: "Beloved, thou doest faithfully whatever thou doest to the brethren, and to strangers; which have borne witness of thy charity before the church: whom if thou bring forward on their journey after a godly sort, thou shalt do well: because that for his name's sake they went forth, taking nothing of the Gentiles. We therefore ought to receive such that we might be fellow helpers to the truth." Rom. 12, 13; Heb. 13, 2; 1 Pet. 4, 9. — Διδακτικόν is **apt to teach,** having the ability, the skill; not: willing to teach, or ready and diligent, as Hofmann understands the word, since the other requirements are all of an ethical kind, not of an educational kind. The adjectives in ικός generally refer to skill: ἀρχικός, apt to rule; ποιητικός, apt to write verse; πρακτικός, able to act; *etc.* Here, then, we have a requirement that must be made of pastors in distinction from laymen. While others frequently possessed extraordinary gifts of the Spirit and might use them for the benefit of the brethren to instruct and teach them, it was required of the leaders of the congregations that they should regularly "feed the church of God, which he hath purchased with his own blood," Acts 20, 28; "labor in the word and in teaching," 1 Tim. 5, 17; hence it was essential that they be "nourished in the words of the faith and of the good doctrine," 4, 6; "give heed to reading," verse 13; and "neglect not the gift that is in thee," verse 14; "take heed to thy teaching," verse 16, its contents and manner; and in particular "hold the pattern of sound words," 2 Tim. 1, 13. Paul himself has put the chief things together: "Preach the word; be instant in season, out of season; reprove, rebuke, exhort, with all longsuffering and doctrine." 2 Tim. 4, 2-3. The requirements in this regard have grown greater, for education has become far more general, and religious error has filled the world. The minister is a public teacher in the church and as such also in the face of the world; unless he is able to teach the Word of God in an efficient manner, it would be a calamity to give him this responsible office.

(3) **No brawler, no striker; but gentle, not contentious, no lover of money.**

First five personal qualifications; then two connected directly with the office and the pastor's relation to Christians in general and to his own flock in particular; now five more which deal with his conduct in its wider scope within and without the congregation. As men deal with him in sacred and secular affairs, they are never to find him a **brawler,** or as the margin renders the word: "quarrelsome over wine." And we must add the next statement: μὴ πλήκτην, **no striker,** quick with his fists, ready to resort to violence. Paul was not a prohibitionist in the modern sense of the word, he himself urged to use a little wine (5, 7), and nowhere do we find that Christians as such or pastors as regards their holy office are to abstain from the proper use of intoxicant drinks. But the apostle is thoroughly opposed to every kind of abuse of this, or any other, Christian liberty. He has no use for a man in the ministry who frequents taverns, sits at the wine (πάροινον, from παρά, beside, and οἶνος, wine), lets it cloud his brain and inflame his anger in argument, so that violence may result. Mosheim writes that the taverns of that day were exceedingly bad — and it seems they have not improved in our beautiful America even in this twentieth century. Hofmann interprets that a pastor must not be a friend of convivial entertainments and revels. — The apostle shows what he means by adding the two opposites: ἀλλὰ ἐπιεικῆ, ἄμαχον, **but gentle, not contentious.** Any excess of drink heats and inflames, and produces violent action; anything of this sort is disgraceful in any Christian, and it certainly disqualifies for leadership in the church. Whether in connection with wine or not, a bishop's temper must always be under control, and in dealing with men he must be mild, fair, "gentle" in voice and act, willing to yield where in conscience he can, not violently insisting on what he deems is right. "Not contentious" means that he keep out of quarrels and strife, loving peace and working for it at all times. — The apostle rounds out the qualifications pertaining to the pastor's conduct in general among men, by adding: **no lover of money,** ἀφιλάργυρον. The A. V. inserts from Tit. 1, 7: μὴ αἰσχροκερθῆ, "not greedy of filthy lucre," before ἀλλά, disturbing the balance of the apostle's thought by duplicating it in the wrong place. We may take ἀφιλάργυρον by itself — a preacher who is "after the money" is very blameworthy in the eyes of Christians and of men generally. But we may heed also the setting in which the word here occurs:

gentle — not contentious — not avaricious. He is not to strive and quarrel about money, pay, profit, and the like; this would reveal his love of money and end his usefulness in the holy ministry. How necessary also this part of the apostle's specifications are we see at the present day: ministers speculate; allow themselves to be persuaded to make investments which promise tremendous financial returns; become agents and solicitors for such concerns among their own people and brethren; allow themselves to be dazzled by high salaries; show themselves niggardly toward the work of the church; take undue legal advantage; *etc.* The church is not built where the love of money rules. This love itself must be quenched and in place of it we must put the love of souls. Preachers often imagine that they are making great financial sacrifices by serving the Lord in the ministry, foregoing the great incomes they might have in other callings or labors; the ministry has its own supreme rewards when rightly followed, and he who prefers to these the riches of mere secular gain ought by all means to step out of his holy service and go "into business," where he may pile up his thousands — perhaps! Note that at the one end of this line of five requirements Paul places drink, at the other money; he has associated these two elsewhere, 1 Cor. 6, 10. To show us the better how this pair looks let us remember that covetousness is usually associated with the twin sin of drink, namely sexual impurity, Eph. 5, 3; Rom. 1, 29; *etc.*

(4) **One that ruleth well his own house, having** *his* **children in subjection with all gravity;** (5) **(but**

if a man knoweth not how to rule his own house, how shall he take care of the church of God?).

The apostle connects the entire private life of the pastor with his holy office. In secular pursuits this may be different; an employer may care little what his employees do outside of their working hours, although here too vices and faults do not make for efficiency in service. But he who would direct the spiritual affairs of men must himself be spiritually fit in all respects. We do not know whether Timothy himself had a family, but we do know that the apostle reckoned chiefly with married men in the ministry, men with families, wife, children, and possibly servants. And he insisted that in these families the normal relation should obtain, as both nature and grace intend it. A bishop must be **one that ruleth well his own house.** The emphasis is on ἰδίου and καλῶς, on both of which the following deduction turns. The pres. mid. part. προϊστάμενον, like the following act. aor. inf. προστῆναι, means to govern, direct, manage, *vorstehen,* to be at the head of. The husband and father is to be the head of the family, not merely nominally, but in fact. Here the relation to his children is the vital thing; τέκνα is without the article, referring thus to any children a pastor may have. The apostle, as Wohlenberg points out, is not requiring something of the children of pastors, but of these pastors themselves; so the thought is not: that he have children, and that these be obedient; but that he hold them in obedience or subjection. Meyer objects to this meaning of ἔχειν, but it is ἔχειν ἐν that is so used, comp. Rom. 1, 28: ἔχειν ἐν ἐπιγνώσει, to hold or retain (God) in their knowledge. So a pastor is to illustrate the fourth commandment in his own family by acting the part of a careful Christian father in training his children to proper obedience. The addition **with all gravity** or dignity goes best with "ruleth well his own house," as applying to his entire position as head of the family; to refer it to the children, that they be obedient "in all gravity," as Meyer thinks best, is to make the apostle again lay duties upon the children instead of the father, and one that does not befit their age and station. The restriction which Meyer then adds, that this pertains to older children, betrays that he is wrong. Paul wants no Eli in the ministry, condoning the disobedience and wickedness of his children. But the best training and care are sometimes unavailing; a wayward son or daughter may in spite of it bring shame and disgrace upon a Christian pastor. As long as it is plain that his own carelessness is not the cause, however deplorable this result, he is not to be blamed, nor will right thinking people blame him. It is his own inability or dereliction which would cause offense. — But the apostle has more in mind than any evil effect of a pastor's wrong example, however serious this already would be. There is a graver side to the matter: how shall such a man **take care of the church of God,** which the apostle himself calls a "house" in verse 15. Lack of ability to rule in the smaller household argues for the same lack in ruling a larger and more important household; carelessness regarding his own children cannot but imply a like fault in managing the members of his congregation who are placed in filial relation to him and over whom he is to exercise paternal care. The argument is *a minori ad majus,* and Bengel puts it rightly: *plus est regere ecclesiam, quam familiam.* Only in drawing out the argument the apostle is careful to use instead of "rule" the lesser word "take care of," ἐπιμελέομαι. But this only makes the point at issue stronger: such a pastor would be unfit even to take care of the church, to say nothing of ruling it; for in other connections the latter term is used also of congregations: οἱ προεστῶτες πρεσβύτεροι, 1 Tim. 5, 17; comp. Heb. 13, 17. The apostle does not use the stronger term here because the rule of a father over his children is not entirely parallel with the rule of a pastor over the flock; the members are not children, the pastor is only called to his position and may lay down his office or be called elsewhere. But as long as he holds the pastoral office in any congregation, we must have reasonable assurance that he is both competent and conscientious enough to take care of the church of God — so precious a trust because belonging to God. This care will include many things: administering with faithfulness and diligence the Word and the sacraments, in public and in private, especially also correcting the wayward, restraining the foolish, rebuking the obstinate — all this and much besides so that if possible not a single one be lost. One of the essential requirements in a pastor must ever be that he show himself worthy of the confidence which his people by virtue of their call place in him. For a minister to forfeit this confidence is to forfeit the right to his office under his call.

(6) **Not a novice, lest being puffed up he fall into the condemnation of the devil.**

The original construction: δεῖ εἶναι with the accusative still continues, the preceding sentence being in the nature of a parenthesis. Paul mentions first five personal qualifications; next two qualifications connected with the office; then a few important points of conduct in dealing with men, verse 3; finally, verses 4-7, three considerations that affect the confidence the church necessarily must have in its pastor. The second of these is that he must not be **a novice,** μὴ νεόφυτον, one freshly grown, just recently brought to the Christian faith. A man of this sort almost always lacks the wisdom which comes with training and experience. Paul himself was called at the time of his conversion, but God himself qualified him in an immediate manner; we to-day call young men into the ministry, but only after they have been properly trained and fitted out. A novice is unfit because he is prone to become conceited; τυφωθείς, the passive in an intransitive sense: **puffed up.** The verb τυφόω signifies to wrap in smoke, to make dull or senseless, and the passive to be wrapped in clouds of conceit and folly, to be silly or vain. — The result will be that **he fall into the condemnation of the devil.** Luther was not positive in regard to τοῦ διαβόλου, translating it with *Laesterer,* slanderer. The word is really an adjective turned into a noun by means of the article, and is then used regularly of the devil; thus, beyond a doubt, in the following verse, but in verse 11 and elsewhere without the article in the general sense "slanderous." The difficulty in our passage is to determine the force of the genitive as appended to κρίμα: judgment (here, as generally, adverse: **condemnation**) of the devil. If the judgment is meant that came upon the devil, when he vaunted himself in pride, we would expect the article with κρίμα; and then Paul's statement would appear extreme in its severity. The other and preferable alternative is to read the genitive as subjective: the judgment which the devil pronounces. Bengel has frightened the commentators by his remark: *Diabolus potest opprobrium inferre, judicium inferre not potest; non enim judicat, sed judicatur.* In the absolute sense this is true; God alone judges. Nevertheless, the devil as a slanderer *arrogates* to himself judgment against us, whenever he has the least opportunity. The conceit of neophytes in the ministry would furnish him exactly what he desires. As a slanderer he would delight to find occasion or cause to utter condemnation upon them. Of course, he would use human instruments for his purpose, and there would be no lack of such. Let every minister remain duly humble and cling to the Word as his only guide; let especially every beginner in the work realize that the devil is dogging his steps.

(7) **Moreover he must have good testimony from them that are without; lest he fall into reproach and the snare of the devil.**

No congregation can have proper confidence in a novice, nor can it have such confidence in a man who has a bad report among men outside of the church. The δεῖ of verse 2 is now finally repeated, with δέ in the sense of "moreover," adding something that differs from the previous statement. What Paul now says is really the positive side of the first requirement laid down, thus closing the circle and completing the whole: on the negative side a bishop must be "blameless," which for the positive side means he must have "good testimony," μαρτυρίαν καλήν, from those without. His past life must be clean and void of offense, so that people generally, when they speak the truth, speak well of him. Of course, evil tongues may besmirch the reputation even of a good man, but the apostle is not referring to such; οἱ ἔξωθεν are the public generally in distinction from the congregation. If people without are justified in charging a man with moral dereliction, he is rendered unfit for the ministry. And this is usually the case even when he has repented of his sin, amended his life, and received the forgiveness of the congregation. Those without have nothing to do with these matters of Christian discipline, they judge only in the ordinary human way, and do not soon forget or overlook grave moral faults. A man who has been guilty of things of this kind generally loses his standing and influence in a community for a long time. He should not aspire to the ministry, and if in it should step out. — **Lest he fall** *etc.* states what the apostle intends to have avoided. Meyer prefers to connect τοῦ διαβόλου only with παγίδα, not also with ὀνειδισμόν; but his reason is insufficient, namely 1 Tim. 5, 4 which in no way decides the matter. While the verb stands between the two nouns, there is but one preposition for both, and the sense of both nouns admits of the appended genitive. The devil loves a shining mark; he delights in doing damage to the ministry, because this always injures the church severely. **Reproach** here is not slander, false charges and the like, it is the opposite of "good testimony" and may be based altogether on truth. Satan would delight to use every just cause for reproach against a minister, he certainly would make the most of it, using as his tools those without, and possibly also some within the church. — Παγίς is a **snare** for catching birds or beasts. The devil is a cunning hunter, and would use any past moral derelictions of a minister to bring about, if possible, his complete undoing. The word suggests temptation and seduction, with the possible result of complete destruction; compare 6, 9; 2 Tim. 2, 26; Rom. 11, 9. Just how this "snare" would operate Paul does not say; some think that the common reproach and disgrace might affect the man so as to undermine his faith and attachment to the Christian religion, and thus turn him at last altogether to unbelief and an unchristian life. There are indeed examples of this kind, where public shame pushed a man down lower and lower. But the lack of a good report may prove a snare in another way; having lost this valuable asset already, a man may listen the more readily to other evil suggestions of the devil, and thus become ensnared anew and more fatally than ever. Von Gerlach's advice is good: Let every Christian who has turned away from past reproachful conduct seek retirement, and prove by his deeds what he now confesses, and let him not try to fill public positions. — Stellhorn, *Die Pastoralbriefe Pauli,* I, 71, makes the following practical deductions on this subject: During the times of the beginning, from which our letter grew, the question evidently was at first concerning men who were *to be chosen* to the office, and with these the church had to deal in certain respects more strictly than with men who are already in office; for it is easier, without appearing to be harsh and unloving, to keep a man from entering the ministry, than to remove him from the office. What may suffice to accomplish the former with due justice, does not always suffice to accomplish the latter in good conscience. When we compare what a man has to his credit with what he may lack, the former must outweigh the latter to a considerable extent, in order that we may permit him, except in time of great need for the church, to enter the ministry; but when we proceed to remove a man from the office without harshness and offense, the balance between these two must be reversed.

HOMILETICAL HINTS.

A sermon on the ministry is a good thing for almost any congregation. The one on this text ought to have the great διάκονος and δοῦλος, who himself penned the text, behind it. At the same time it ought to be centered upon the congregation, whose welfare and spiritual interest Paul had before his eyes when he wrote his pastoral Epistles, in particular also the words of our text. While Paul was not the permanent minister of any one congregation, but one who moved from place to place to establish congregations, he after all only began what he expected others to take over from his hands and continue on exactly the same lines and for exactly the same great purpose for which he had begun it. There are things in the office of an apostle which no other man can repeat, and we see also that the Lord called no other apostles to succeed those he first chose; but there are many sides to the work of an apostle which were to be repeated, and are repeated to this day, and for all of these the one apostle whom we know best in his work in the churches, because we have the fullest record concerning it all, must ever be for us a mine of information and a source of inspiration. While then an apostle had to have very special qualifications, he also had to have those qualifications which his successors in the different congregations had to have to continue his work successfully. The specifications which Paul thus laid down for bishops and elders in the church applied very largely to himself, so that we can see from Paul's letter how he conceived this side of his great office and work and in his own person met fully the requirements laid down by himself. There is really only one point which receives no light from the apostle's own conduct; it is that he, for special reasons, did not marry and rear a family. But even here let us remember 1 Cor. 9, 5 (R. V.) : "Have we no right to lead about a wife that is a believer, even as the rest of the apostles, and the brethren of the Lord, and Cephas?" So this point is also easily taken care of.

J. Warneck writes (*Paulus,* 202) : "The pastoral letters permit us to feel what the apostle must have been for his helpers. Here speaks the master who was concerned just as much about the purity of his congregation as about the proving of his sons in whom he renewed his youth. The experience which he had purchased in the midst of bitter sufferings and disappointments he wanted to make fruitful for those whom he loved. With anxiety in his heart he points to the dangers which threaten them in their youthfulness in the midst of an obstinate generation. Thinking of his paternal love we may excuse him for making his admonitions to his tried fellow laborers somewhat extensive. One can readily understand a man's solicitude for beloved pupils surrounded by many temptations. Sometimes a missionary to-day meets in fellow workers, upon whom he had built great hopes, and whom as his tried friends he deemed in the harbor of safety, bitter disappointment (Demas, 2 Tim. 4, 10)."

Why all these requirements of ministers? For their own sakes, because of their own great personal responsibility; for their work's sake, because this is the highest and holiest work in the world; for their congregation's sake, because the congregation exists, not for the benefit of the minister, but the minister and his entire calling for the benefit of the congregation. As Jesus loved the church and gave himself for it, so in his lesser office and calling Paul loved the church and devoted his life to it, and so must every minister in the position assigned to him manifest a similar love and devotion and give himself heart and soul to his work.

Piety assumes an aspect somewhat different, in different ages and periods of the church. There is in human nature a strong tendency to extremes. In one age, or community, the leaning is to enthusiasm; in another to superstition. At one time, religion is made to assume a severe and gloomy aspect. At such times, all cheerfulness is proscribed; and the Christian whom nature prompts to smile, feels a check from the monitor within. The religious habits of some serious professors of religion are adapted to make a very unfavorable impression on the minds of sensible men. They assume a demure and sanctimonious air, and speak in an affected and drawling tone; often sighing and lifting up their eyes, and giving utterance to ejaculations. Now these may be truly pious, but the impression made on most minds by this affectation is, that they are hypocrites, who aim at being thought uncommonly devout. Religion never appears so lovely as when she wears the dress of perfect simplicity. Men of the world form their opinions of the nature of piety from what they observe in its professors, and from such exhibitions often take up prejudices that are never removed. Alexander.

What a homely set of virtues this list of the apostle puts down for ministers! Let us remember that Paul was himself a healthy, robust, work-a-day Christian and minister. He wore no halo. And experience has taught abundantly that the very men who cultivate a peculiar odor of sanctity and saintliness in the ministry, surrounding themselves with a circle of adoring friends and worshippers, are most likely to be brought to a fall by the cunning of the devil, who seems to take a special delight in besmirching their self-made holiness with some sin or other of a very unsaintly odor.

Does this set of virtues look easy to you, my fellow pastor, my fellow Christian? Be thankful that the Lord did not require more. Many a pastor has failed to secure a high grade in these common branches in the school of his ministerial life, and some have failed. Is it always easy to get a hundred in gentleness, when so many things in the church and its members provoke us? Or in temperate judgment, when some fly to this and others to that extreme? Or in humility, when men flatter us and the devil secretly nourishes our pride? Or in unselfishness, when we feel the lack of money while others are far better paid and the devil tries to make us pull wires for a better paying place? Or in the management of our own children, when their very position as the pastor's children and the foolishness of our parishioners tends to make them bold and forward? On the point of humility remember Luther whom somebody once praised inordinately for the very excellent sermon he had just preached; he replied that that was exactly what the devil whispered into his ear as he came down the pulpit steps. And on the point of unselfishness — how many ministers do you suppose are ready to accept harder places than they happen to have or places with poorer pay? Even levity, and that in sacred things, is not such a rare fault among the clergy.

Apt to teach means, not only by precept, but also by practice. Intellectual knowledge is easy to impart, especially where pupils are bright; but heart knowledge, spiritual knowledge, is quite another thing. Stop with the brain and you have only reached the threshold; to reach the will you must go much further, and this always requires of the spiritual teacher that his own will shall have been reached and fully anchored by faith in the truth.

Apt to teach includes those chapters of the Christian life which in our times happen to be unpopular. Some of the great lights in the church fail to cast even a glimmer upon this or that great and dangerous popular error or deadly entanglement of sin. Have you noted how revivalists carefully omit certain sins and errors, while they ride others to death? Paul taught the whole counsel of God and kept his hands clean of the blood of all men. Be a Pauline bishop also in this respect! the world has never needed such more than it needs them today. Secretism is more deadly to souls than drunkenness; unionism more dangerous than theft.

With all his requirements Paul wants what he fully succeeded in attaining in himself: wholehearted sincerity. He himself was what he preached and professed, and all that he preached he preached first to himself, then to others. His official position and life were identical with his personal position and life, and both were in complete unity with the Word and will of his Lord. He has had many successors who, if they had been honest, would have had to say to their people, as one is reported actually to have said: Do as I tell you, not as you may see me do! It is easy to lay burdens upon others and the while to forget that thereby these burdens are laid also upon us. The professional attitude of many a man pronounces the verdict of guilt upon his private attitude. How little true sincerity lies back of many a preacher's work is revealed when for some reason or other a preacher quits his work; he then suddenly throws off the mask and does and says things he has himself condemned publicly perhaps for years. His own hollowness is a greater curse to himself than his unmasking is an offense to others.

St. Paul, a Minister of Ministers.

I. *What he taught with the word of truth,*
   1) Regarding the minister's personal character; 2) his work in the congregation; 3) and his general conduct among men,
II. *That he sealed with the example of his own life.*
   1) The marks of his character; 2) his work in the church; 3) his life and influence among men generally.

The Christian Ministry: The Work and The Workers.

I. *The kind of workers this work demands.*
II. *The kind of work these workers do.*

Who is Concerned in the Christian Ministry?

I. *God and the church.*
   1) God has established both the church and the ministry.
   2) The ministry is to be a "good work" in maintaining, upbuilding, extending the church. (Example: St. Paul, Timothy.)
   3) God wants men well qualified for this work, and the church can prosper only when it has such servants.

II. *The ministers themselves.*
   1) They must meet the requirements made by God (as did Paul and Timothy).
   2) They must efficiently and successfully perform the work (responsibility).
   3) They have in the work well done an imperishable reward.

III. *The devil and the world.*
   1) They are bound to antagonize the ministry.
   2) They will use any opportunity the ministry affords them.

St. Paul Shows us the Qualities of a True Christian Minister.

I. *As to his own person.*
   1) He is to be free from vices and passions.
   2) He is to possess the virtues that will endear him to his fellow men.
   3) He must have the ability to teach.
   4) He must be no novice in the faith, in order that he may speak from experience.

II. *As to his home life.*
   1) The husband of one wife — a model for Christian marriage.
   2) The wife is to manifest a Christian spirit.
   3) The parents are to train their children in godliness and uprightness.
   4) The home is to be well managed, so that nothing in it may rob the minister of respect.

III. *As to his calling.*
   1) He is to be blameless as concerns non-Christians, unbelievers, men of other faiths, in order that his work may not suffer because of deserved reproach.
   2) But for the sake of his work he is to suffer shame willingly, as long as he is innocent of guilt.

Lisco.

The Greatest Work in the Church.

I. *Its great excellence.*
   1) Eternal treasures are committed to the ministry:
      a) In preaching and in teaching to enlighten men's souls.
      b) In the sacraments to receive souls into the church and to confirm them in the Christian life.
      c) In the care of souls, to save the erring and to strengthen the weak.
   2) A minister must, therefore, center all his thoughts upon divine things, past, present, and future, and must depend for temporal things upon the love of his congregation.

II. *Its great difficulties.*
   1) A minister must be as complete an example as possible for his people, though he is but a weak man himself: "blameless."
   2) And all this not only once, for a little while, but always and in all respects, turning all his thoughts to further the glory of God and the welfare of his people; for if he fails to do this, how can he demand it of others?

Wfg.

THE APOSTLE OF HOPE.
1 Cor. 15, 42b-49.

Among the grand chapters of the Bible First Corinthians fifteen holds its assured place. Its one great theme is the resurrection from the dead, and in elaborating it the apostle takes up some questions which, if at all, are touched on only slightly in other portions of Scripture. Some of its sections have become standard texts for preaching purposes, and a number of passages are in our catechisms for our children to memorize. It was St. Paul who penned this chapter by divine inspiration. Intended first of all to fit the special needs of his congregation at Corinth, where philosophical and rationalistic doubt concerning the resurrection had arisen, it has in reality met the needs of the entire church of all ages in its constant conflict with doubt and unbelief concerning man's future state. Here shines the great sun of Christian hope in Jesus Christ the risen Savior, with rays so refulgent that all darkening shadows and depressing mists must flee before it. As we individually come nearer and nearer to death and the grave this chapter helps us on to a glorious victory and an eternal triumph. Its mighty comfort upholds and cheers us as we stand beside the graves of our loved ones who have died in the faith. Tongue cannot tell nor pen record the streams of blessings which have flowed out from this one portion of Scripture alone.

What Paul here wrote was the basis of his own

hope in death, the grave, and eternity. In trying to learn to know the apostle better we thus keep together his own person and the great doctrine he was sent to teach to all the world. This personal touch ought to make the doctrine more precious than ever to us personally. Here is a man who lived with death often at his side, but his step was firm, his eye bright, because his way was all lit up and made beautiful by the light of divine revelation. In this too he surely serves as our example. He is indeed the apostle of justification by *faith*, and the thirteenth chapter of our Epistle shows him also as the apostle of *love;* but surely this fifteenth chapter rounds out the trio, entitling him in a marked degree to be called in addition the apostle of *hope*.

The selection from the chapter here offered as a text is one less frequently usd, but altogether characteristic of Paul in general and of the way he writes in this chapter. The usual pericope embraces verses 35-49, Paul's proof that there is a vast difference in created bodies, and that thus it is folly to conclude, because our bodies are now grossly material, they cannot be made to exist in an entirely different and far higher state. All the world of created things cries out against such blindness of human wisdom, and all the world of divine revelation mightily assures us of the contrary. The verses which constitute our text present the elaborate summary of this line of thought by placing in contrast to each other what our bodies now are as they die and turn to dust, and what our bodies presently shall be through Christ in the glorious resurrection to come.

(15, 42) . . . **It is sown in corruption; it is**

1 Cor. 15, 42b-49.

raised in incorruption: (43) **it is sown in dishonor; it is raised in glory: it is sown in weakness; it is raised in power:** (44) **it is sown a natural body; it is raised a spiritual body.**

St. Paul admits to the fullest degree all that men of his day, or for that matter of any day, are able to say concerning the gross earthly and perishable nature of our mortal bodies. He knew thoroughly what his own body was made of, and what its fate would be in the grave which awaited it. But instead of using this basis of truth for arguing downward with a false show of human logic and wisdom, he uses it to argue upward with the divine wisdom and logic of God's revelation concerning his unlimited power. And the apostle proceeds concretely, not theoretically; he has ordinary people in mind; he wants all to know, understand, and believe. What a difference among the bodies we see, created by God's omnipotent power. What a transformation wrought in some of these now already before our very eyes, for instance when the bare seed of wheat is given a wonderfully new body in the slender, graceful stalk of wheat — something we would deem utterly impossible did we not see it occur in nature a thousand times. And what a difference in the beauty and glory of many of these bodies as we now behold them, God giving to one what far transcends his gift to another. He who has done this, and still constantly does it, works with a similar power in the resurrection from the dead, taking our vile body and, without giving us another in its stead, making this very body something exceedingly more glorious in the state that awaits us at the last day. — Thus, then, the apostle unfolds the grand conclusion he has had in mind all along: **It is sown in corruption; it is raised in incorruption.** Daechsel is correct when he says that Paul now weaves together the figurative expressions he has used, with plain statements of the reality, and this in beautiful symmetry, one statement naturally following another, until the whole thought in rounded form is before our minds. Σπείρεται goes back to σπείρεις in verse 36 and the important imagery there connected with the word; over against it, here and in the following, is set with dramatic emphasis ἐγείρεται. The apparent contrast, sowing down into the ground and raising up out of it, is reenforced by a veiled contrast, which appears the moment the matter is considered a little carefully: both verbs are passives, but the agent in the one is man, in the other God. How Wohlenberg can say that verse 36 with its σύ suggests for σπείρεται in our passage God as the agent, is hard to see, since ἄφρων, σὺ ὃ σπείρεις, "thou foolish one, that which thou thyself sowest," is so strongly and exclusively human. Moreover, this figure of sowing into the ground, when Paul now uses the same word in stating the thought directly, must signify the burial of the dead human body. It is true enough that our bodies are all along subject to the law of **corruption,** φθορά (Besser, Hofmann, Daechsel), "constantly tending to decay, subject to disease and death, and destined to entire dissolution" (Hodge); but Paul is not speaking of this power of corruption and any manifestation of it in general, but in particular of a *sowing* in corruption. Strictly speaking this means laying the dead body into its last resting place, the grave. The apostle thus mentions the supreme result of the whole process of corruption, and by keeping close to his thought we lose nothing whatever, we only gain: as we see the dead body lowered into the grave, and fix our eyes upon this one strange act of sowing, we have at the same time a vision like nothing else could give us of the entire corrupting process that has led up to this significant point. — **In corruption** = in a condition of corruption; the body filled with corruption, marked and characterized by it, is laid into the ground. Decay, disintegration, putrefaction have taken hold of it; this is the work of death upon the human body, and there is nothing pleasant about it, it is ugly, terrible, shocking. — Now the tremendous contrast: "it is raised in incorruption." The subject is left indefinite as in the previous sentence, but purposely so, it makes the whole presentation, so brief and compact, reduced down to the bare essentials in the case, the more dramatic and telling. That which is sown, the dead body, not something else, some new body, newly created, **is raised,** by the omnipotent power of him who has promised us the resurrection. "Raised" — when? At the last day, when God shall call us forth from our sleep in the grave. The mention of different kinds of bodies in the previous verses, men, beasts, birds, fish, celestial and terrestrial, sun, moon, stars, and different stars, dare not be urged, in the application which Paul makes of this extended analogy, to shut out the identity of the body sown in death and raised in the resurrection. The point of the analogy is only in the difference, for different spheres of existence. This difference, as seen by our eyes in a variety of bodies, illustrates what God does for our mortal bodies, when he raises them from corruption to incorruption, putting them into an entirely new and different state of existence, as befits the new sphere he makes them enter. — **Incorruption,** ἀφθαρσία, is the opposite of corruption, a condition absolutely removed from, and exalted above, all decay, disintegration, and dissolution. When God raises our bodies from the grave they will be in this new, glorious, heavenly condition. He who made the glory of the sun, so different from the qualities of mere clay and dust, will give our bodies a glory like that, though once they were but clay and dust and lay in the earth as such.

But more must be said, for there are other sides to this great truth. **It is sown in dishonor,** again at the time of burial; ἐν ἀτιμίᾳ, all its previous loveliness and attractiveness gone, though now we deck the corpse with flowers and try to hold yet for a little the fair appearance it had in life. Worms shall devour it; an intolerable stench shall emanate from it (John 11, 39); it must be covered from the sight of men. A monument may ornament the grave, within are only a dead man's bones. — But **it is raised in glory,** the same body, when God at last calls it forth; all the "dishonor" gone, and "glory" is now in its place, namely a resplendent beauty, loveliness, brightness, a shining excellence which arouses admiration and delight in all who behold it. Then shall our bodies be fashioned like unto the glorious body of Christ himself, Phil. 3, 21. "Transparent as crystal the body of the resurrection will radiate the glory which the Spirit of Christ imparts to it; the flesh, no longer a dull covering, will be a lamp of spiritual light, like as Jesus was glorified upon the holy mount." Besser. — And yet again: **it is sown in weakness,** ἀσθένεια, in utter lack of σθένος or strength, able to do nothing, and to resist nothing — a mere inert clod. What little strength the body did have in the short time of its earthly life is gone, utterly gone; it is now nothing but a helpless prey of the natural elements. — But again the contrast; **it is raised in power,** to a new life, the mark of which for the body is δύναμις, power in the sense of ability and strength to do things, power as manifested in mighty action. The resurrection will bestow upon our bodies an energy consonant with the new, heavenly abode God has prepared for them, and this energy will go forth in a corresponding activity. It is an addition of human thought when Grotius adds: *cum sensibus multis quos nunc non intelligimus*. We may try to imagine what our δύναμις in the resurrection is to be, but we will not be able now to obtain an adequate conception of it. — **It is sown a natural body,** σῶμα ψυχικόν, which the American Committee of the R. V. wants defined in the margin as "psychial." Paul finally summarizes, by stating now the fundamental constitution of our earthly body, as contrasted with its fundamental constitution in the resurrection and life to come. The term ψυχικόν refers to the ψυχή, the life principle of all bodily animated creatures on earth. The English really has no word for the adjective; the German has *seelisch*. Luther puts it in a strong way: "Natural life is nothing but a bodily life as every beast has it, so that one might indeed call it, in good clear German, a beastly body, *viehisch*." The body that we lay in the grave is one that was controlled by the ψυχή, with a variety of bodily functions and activities. This ψυχή was indeed rational, and thus above the animal, but it was also sinful, and sin invaded to a marked degree the psychial side of our being. Death ends this; when the natural bodily life ceases there is left its inanimate tenement, and this is interred. — At the last day, **it is raised a spiritual body,** σῶμα πνευματικόν; but not a body consisting of πνεῦμα or spirit, for the former was also not a body consisting of the ψυχή, the psychial principle. The whole arrangement and quality of our bodies now is fitted to an earthly existence in a grossly material world. This is true of a Christian also, however much he may rise in his thoughts and acts above earthly things; he eats, drinks, sleeps, wakes, and all his bodily organs and members go on in their functions, the ψυχή having control. In the resurrection it is the πνεῦμα that will have complete control, and the body will be fitted perfectly in every respect to answer to this control. In this sense the body will be πνευματικόν, wholly an organ of the spirit, and this in a world which itself in all its parts and qualities will match the spirit. The Bible does not teach trichotomy, all its statements are in line with dichotomy. Man has a material and an immaterial part. The latter may be named from the lower side, as it is connected with the body; the term then is always ψυχή, not πνεῦμα. But the immaterial part may be named also from its higher side, the one that connects it with God and eternal life; here πνεῦμα is the distinctive term. The work of sin is manifest in the complete control of sin, so that ψυχικὸς ἄνθρωπος (1 Cor. 2, 14) is actually a synonym of carnal, fleshly, unregenerate; the higher side is put altogether out of control. It is the work of the Holy Spirit to make us spiritual again, to bring our entire bodily life into subjection to the πνεῦμα which he has placed in communion with himself and keeps in his control. But while we live in this life there is ever a battle, for this gross sinful world is still about it and we still belong to it. Nor is there a way by which we can be wholly renewed in body, ψυχή, and πνεῦμα, in our material substance, and in both sides of our immaterial substance, so that this conflict will wholly cease in the life on earth. This goal can be reached only through death and a blessed resurrection; then everything which militates against the spirit shall be swept out of our body for good and all, and the ψυχή itself, the life principle that animates this purified body, will be wholly cleansed from any sinful taint or inclination. Thus will the πνεῦμα, joined to the Spirit of God, rule triumphant, and this in a world from which likewise all evil in any and every form will have been removed.

(44) . . . **If there is a natural body, there is also a spiritual** *body*. (45) **So also it is written, The first man Adam became a living soul. The last Adam became a life-giving spirit.**

The *textus receptus* (A. V.) omits εἰ, but the best textual authority requires it. But the conditional form is not meant to express doubt; it has the sense: "If there is a natural body" — and it is plain, admitted on all hands, that there is, for we have it constantly before our eyes. Ἔστιν, accented on the penult, denotes existence: if such a thing as a natural body exists. The conclusion then follows: **there is** (ἔστιν again) **also a spiritual** *body*, the term is not contradictory. If the ψυχή can have, and has, a body adapted to it; why should not the πνεῦμα receive a body at last adapted to it? namely in the resurrection. Now, of course, sin and the curse still affect us, but has not the apostle just spoken of death, and the end of the psychial life? That which shall follow after this, in due time, for all God's children, is the resurrection, and in that renewed body the complete reign of the πνεῦμα, in a body then which well deserves to be called πνευματικόν. So "there is also a spiritual body." — This the apostle substantiates by a Scripture quotation: **So also it is written,** γέγραπται, has been, and now stands written. By this formula he always introduces direct quotations, a point to observe as to the extent of the words here quoted, which comprise only the first sentence: **The first man Adam became a living soul.** The following statement concerning "the last Adam" is of a different nature, it can not be found "written" in so many words like the first. Paul adduces Gen. 2, 7 from the LXX: καὶ ἐγένετο ὁ ἄνθρωπος εἰς ψυχὴν ζῶσαν; the construction ἐγένετο εἰς, instead of a simple nominative, being due to the Hebrew *le: lenephesch chajah*. Paul uses as the subject of his quoted sentence ὁ πρῶτος ἄνθρωπος 'Αδάμ, which is interpretative, and helps to bring out the point of his thought, which is a contrast between Adam and Christ. Adam was created to be a bodily being animated with a living soul, and as such he existed. Even in the state of innocence he required food and sleep. Paul is brief, he uses only this one point and no more; he says nothing of God's intention concerning Adam as first created, of what his body would have become if he had not fallen into sin *etc*. It is enough, we all know Adam from this statement of Scripture as a psychial creature of God, and as ὁ πρῶτος ἄνθρωπος the progenitor of a race like unto himself. — Commentators puzzle about the second sentence: **The last Adam** *became* **a life-giving spirit.** Is this too intended as a quotation? The effort to make it such by pointing to terms like πνοὴν ζωῆς in the LXX (Wohlenberg), or by saying Paul in this sentence gives only in a general way what the Old Test. says of the Messiah, is hardly satisfactory. The words are Paul's own. Yet it is correct that the chief stress is on these words; without them the main point would be without support. Here Meyer's explanation is helpful: the scriptural characterization of Adam, "the first man," is such as silently to involve something, — something concerning "the last Adam," of whom the first was a type. This silent implication Paul puts into plain words for us, words indeed of his own, and not as such a quotation, but words giving us what lies in and beneath the ones literally quoted, as the mind of the Spirit. And we may add that Paul is not thinking merely of the creation of man, at the time God gave him a living soul, but of the inspired record which afterwards God had Moses make of this act, and of the significant words used in making that record. — Ὁ ἔσχατος Ἀδάμ makes Christ the antitype of Adam. Both are progenitors, the one of a psychial race, the other of pneumatical or spiritual. And as it is with all types, the antitype is by far greater, higher, more glorious. — There is no verb in this sentence, ἐγένετο must be understood. Not that the meaning of the word is changed from what it is in the previous sentence; that word is purposely so general in meaning as to have room for what occurred with Christ as well as for what occurred with Adam. Each **became** something, naturally in a way suitable to what each eventually was. — Εἰς πνεῦμα ζωοποιοῦν, **a life-giving spirit,** contains a double contrast; one as between the πνεῦμα of Christ and the ψυχή of Adam; and one as between "life-giving" on Christ's part, and merely "living" on Adam's part. What is meant will be clearer when we determine when this ἐγένετο took place. Some, like Hodge, think of the Incarnation of Christ; others bring in the *communicatio idiomatum*. But Christ in his humiliation assumed a psychic life: "being found in fashion as a man," Phil. 2, 8; he ate, drank, slept, was weary, *etc.*, ἐν ὁμοιώματι σαρκὸς ἁμαρτίας, Rom. 8, 3. Paul also follows up his statement here by several additions which point beyond the Incarnation. It is the glorification that is meant by the ἐγένετο required in this second sentence. With all his redemptive work complete Christ laid aside his humiliation, he for his own humanity assumed a heavenly state; but not merely for himself to live now with his human nature in the most exalted pneumatic state, this nature exercising completely all the divine majesty and power, but to be now for us a source of the heavenly and eternal life. Adam was a **living** soul, and nothing higher is said of him; he is indeed our progenitor, but altogether in a subordinate way, as a mere creature to whom God had given this faculty. Christ is a **life-giving** spirit, he is God himself, he exercises divine power in creating us anew and in being our progenitor in this exalted way. It is simply wonderful with what spiritual skill the words of Holy Writ are placed! So again Adam was a living **soul,** and nothing is said of his spirit, because as our progenitor he communicated to his children nothing but the psychial life, the spiritual, eternal life he did not communicate, having fallen into sin. But Christ is a life-giving **spirit;** he used the psychial life indeed for a time in his great saving purpose, but it is the pneumatic glorified existence of his human nature which is now the source of our spiritual life, and which intends eventually to make us like unto him, even including our body. So each of the terms used has its peculiar and striking connotation and range of meaning. Even Adam received the true life only from Christ. — Paul's introduction of Christ at this point, and this the risen and glorified Christ, will be grasped in its full force when the entire chapter is read, where the resurrection and glorification of Christ is repeatedly brought forward, and this in connection with our own resurrection and eternal salvation. Note especially also toward the close: "But thanks be to God which giveth us the victory through our Lord Jesus Christ."

(46) **Howbeit that is not first which is spiritual, but that which is natural; then that which is spiritual.** (47) **The first man is of the earth, earthy: the second man is of heaven.** (48) **As is the earthy, such are they also that are earthy: and as is the heavenly, such are they also that are heavenly.** (49) **And as we have borne the image of the earthy, we shall also bear the image of the heavenly.**

Verse 46 gives expression to a general law, the exemplification of which then follows. God has so arranged that the higher always follows the lower. Adam's first state was to lead to another, superior to the first. Now we see seed-time first, then the harvest. Even in the work of creation God chose this order. So now spiritually: we are first born, then reborn, then glorified. — Daechsel asks: But is not the soul of man, inbreathed by God, also "of heaven," and the body of Jesus, as conceived by the Virgin, "of the earth?" The answer is that when God created man he took the dust of the earth, and formed his body from that. Man's origin is thus correctly described as ἐκ γῆς; and this origin gives him his character: χοϊκός. He is **of the earth, earthy.** The omission of the article in ἐκ γῆς has no special significance; it is frequent where only one thing or person of a kind exists at all. But ὁ δεύτερος ἄνθρωπος, here evidently Christ our Savior, is ἐξ οὐρανοῦ, for it was the Logos who assumed flesh in the womb of the Virgin. But Paul is not thinking of any fine point as to origin, he is merely stating the order of these two, Adam and Christ, an order which puts the one that is infinitely the greatest, last, not first. "Of the earth, earthy" thus marks Adam's entire character as due to his origin; "of heaven" the character of Christ in his entirety, also as due to his origin. He is the Godman; with everything merely psychial laid aside, with everything "earthy" transformed. When he returns in the glory of heaven with all the angels of God about him we shall see his spiritual body and recognize him in all his glory as supremely ἐξ οὐρανοῦ. Some texts add ὁ κύριος to ὁ δεύτερος ἄνθρωπος; this ought then to be read as an apposition, not as the predicate of the sentence (A. V.); the best reading omits the addition, thus also leaving the sentence simpler.

Paul now makes his application, and we see why he made the previous distinction. **As is the earthy,** namely Adam, having fallen into sin instead of rising without a fall to a higher state, **such are they also that are earthy,** we all who are bodily descendants of Adam and fell in his fall. We all have by nature only a psychial life, the true spiritual life not being transmitted to us by our natural birth. "Earthy" — what a distinction for proud man! His body related to the clods he treads on, and his $\psi v \chi \acute{\eta}$ bent on the things that are connected with these clods. — But thanks be to God, there is deliverance from this death! **As is the heavenly,** namely Christ our Savior in exaltation and glory — an exaltation and glory of his human nature, as the firstborn of many brethren, and as the first fruits of them that sleep, — **such are they also that are heavenly,** Christ's risen followers, their bodies made like unto Christ's own glorious body. "Therefore I may now say to man, as he himself said to Adam: Dust thou art, and to dust thou shalt return. But he is not to remain dust; on the contrary, as before he made of it a beautiful man with body and soul, so again he will make him much more glorious and beautiful. For this reason he now permits him to decay in the earth, that the earthy condition may disappear as by nature perishable only and corruptible, and in addition weak and filthy, and a new man from heaven come forth, who may no longer be termed earthy, but altogether heavenly." Luther. — But the third person does not satisfy Paul, he speaks with a direct personal touch to his Corinthians: **As we have borne the image of the earthy,** namely of Adam — and Besser adds: borne it with a burdened feeling and with homesickness, 2 Cor. 5, 4. Luther: "We have dragged around this heavy body." Paul used the aorist $\dot{\epsilon}\phi o\rho\acute{\epsilon}\sigma a\mu\epsilon\nu$, viewing our entire earthy life as one past event. Φορεῖν is carry or wear constantly, a continuous φέρειν. Here it comes out plainly of whom Paul speaks all along, namely of the true believers, among whom he counts himself. Nothing is said of the rest who resist the Holy Spirit's efforts to convert and regenerate them. Their fate is terrible enough, for all that lies in prospect for the believers is negatived for them. — The weight of textual authority supports the subjunctive φορέσωμεν, "let us hear," which Hofmann defends and Westcott and Hort adopt in their text. But an admonition seems strange in this place, especially also when the thought is kept in mind: to bear **the image of the heavenly,** namely of the heavenly body of Christ in the glorious world to come. We shall be able to begin this bearing only at the end of the world. The admonition is thus shut out by the very subject-matter itself, and in spite of the authorities we must read φορέσομεν: **we shall bear.** The word is a glorious promise, behind which stands the glorious Savior himself who will make it good. We who in our poor earthy bodies bear the likeness of earthy Adam and carry it even into the grave, shall there exchange, not indeed our bodies as such — these like our immaterial part belong to our being and identity, — but our likeness, trading the old for a new one when these same bodies rise from the dead at the call of the last trumpet. — All through this text there runs an exceptional vigor and wealth of thought in proof and deduction, which is marked by the absence of connecting particles, otherwise so necessary to the Greek mind.

HOMILETICAL HINTS.

In this text too Paul and his words belong together. So again we see the hidden power that made his life so strong and rich: he believed fully and completely the Savior's promise of the resurrection of the dead. In the light of the great beyond he did his daily work. He measured all earthly things with the heavenly standard; thus he knew them for what they really were, and freed his mind from false estimates. He put his work where it counted most, aiming at results that would endure beyond the short day of our temporal life. He had not only cast off the fear of death, as some falsely imagine they have done, he had put in its place the great heavenly hope in Christ, which gives the soul in all earthly labors, trials, and sufferings a heavenly poise and mastery which nothing merely human can bestow. He bore the hard image of the earthly as one destined at last, in the image of the heavenly, to walk with angels and the spirits of just men made perfect in the heavenly presence of the Lord. The nobility of the great apostle's life and work is not fully seen until this hope lights up our own hearts.

The Exposition of the Bible has the following: By the hope of the life beyond Paul had been induced to undergo the greatest privations in this life. He had been exposed to countless dangers and indignities. Although a Roman citizen, he had been cast into the arena to contend with wild beasts: there was no risk he had not run, no hardship he had not endured. But in all he was sustained by the assurance that there remained for him a rest and an inheritance in a future life. Remove this assurance and you remove the assumption on which his conduct is wholly built. If there is no future life either to win or to lose, then the Epicurean motto may take the place of Christ's promise, "Let us eat and drink, for tomorrow we die." — It may indeed be said that even if there be no life to come, this life is best spent in the service of man, however full of hazard and hardship that service be. That is quite true; and had Paul believed this life was all, he might still have chosen to spend it, not on sensual indulgence, but in striving to win men to something better. But in that case there would have been no deception and no disappointment. In point of fact, however, Paul believed in a life to come, and it was because he believed in that life he gave himself to the work of winning men to Christ regardless of his own pains and losses. And what he says is that if he is mistaken, then all these pains and losses have been gratuitous, and that his whole life has proceeded on a mistake. The life to which he sought to win, and for which he sought to prepare men, does not exist.

In the apocryphal Book of Wisdom we read: "Our life is short and tedious, and in the death of man is no remedy; neither was any man ever known to return from the grave: for we are all born at an adventure, and shall be afterwards as though we had never been; for the breath of our nostrils is as smoke, and a little spark is the moving of our heart, which, being extinguished, our bodies will be burnt to ashes, and our spirit vanish as the soft air: and our name shall be forgotten in time, and no man shall hold our works in remembrance, and our life shall pass away like the trace of a cloud, and shall be dispersed as a mist that is driven away with the beams of the sun, and overcome with the heat thereof. . . . Come on, therefore, let us enjoy the good things that are present, and let us speedily use the creatures like as in youth. Let us fill ourselves with costly wine and ointments, and let no flower of the spring pass us by; let us crown ourselves with rosebuds before they be withered; let none of us go without his share of voluptuousness; let us leave tokens of our joyfulness in every place, for this is our portion, and our lot is this." — This would indeed be man's true philosophy if this life were all.

Within the world once created not a single atom is ever annihilated; the original substances of which the body now decayed consisted, thus still exist, and the Omniscient knows where they are, and the Almighty is able to gather them again. But in the meantime they, together with the world of nature in which they are preserved, have experienced the process of fire, from which heaven and earth come forth in lucid glorification: out of this glorified world he who originally formed the body of man out of the earth of Eden, will bring the original substance of our bodies forth again, with the same arrangement of powers woven through them, and the same combination of essential parts, as far as this arrangement and combination, after the removal of sin with its presuppositions and results, condition the individuality that remains; and the soul, brought into union again with this bodily form, will take possession of it, as a queen of her throne, penetrate it with its heavenly light, and make it a translucid manifestation of its spiritual being, and will unite itself with this body as the goal of its longing in the undivided perfection of its personality. Delitzsch.

The resurrection of the body Luther in the Apostles' Creed called the resurrection of the flesh, meaning the material body of flesh; but in the resurrection this body of flesh will no longer be flesh in the sense of corruptible mortal flesh, for the flesh of our body will then put on incorruption and glory.

The notion that our earthly body when laid in the grave will decay and remain in decay, and that from it there will grow and blossom out in the resurrection a germ, not this body itself, but in some way now hidden in it, is itself a corruption of the divine truth, a perversion of the Lord's promise. So also the idea that not our mortal body of clay and dust, but this peculiar germ, implanted in us by regeneration, and fed and kept alive by the spiritual food of the Holy Supper, is to be brought forth in the resurrection. Our entire bodies are now the temple of God, and shall remain his temple to all eternity. Paul in other places argues from the body as God's temple to the individual parts and members of this body, as equally holy with the entire body, and because integral parts of it. Sanctification now embraces our body with all its constituent members, and in the same way glorification will embrace all our members. These our very eyes will see God, and this our very skin will enfold us when we see him. Nothing less is our Christian hope, and no refinement of human speculation dare take its place.

A great part of the temptations of this present life arise from the conditions in which we necessarily exist as dependent for our comfort in great measure on the body. And one can scarcely conceive the feeling of emancipation and superiority which will possess those who have no anxiety about a livelihood, no fear of death, no distraction of appetite.

Human nature is a thing of immense possibilities and range. On the one side it is akin to the lower animals, to the physical world and all that is in it, high and low; on the other side it is akin to the highest of all spiritual existences, even to God himself. At present we are in a world admirably adapted for our probation and discipline, a world in which, in point of fact, every man does attach himself to the lower or to the higher, to the present or to the eternal, to the natural or to the spiritual. And though the results of this may not be apparent in average cases, yet in extreme cases the results of human choice are obtrusively apparent. Let a man give himself unrestrainedly and exclusively to animal life in its grosser forms, and the body itself soon begins to suffer. You can see the process of physical deterioration going on, deepening in misery until death comes. But what follows death? Can one promise himself or another a future body which shall be exempt from the pains which unrepented sin produced? Are those who have by their vice committed a slow suicide to be clothed hereafter in an incorruptible and efficient body? It seems wholly contrary to reason to suppose so. And how can their probation be continued if the very circumstance which makes this life so thorough a probation to us all — the circumstance of our being clothed with a body — is absent? The truth is, there is no subject on which more darkness hangs or on which Scripture preserves so ominous a silence as the future of the body of those who in this life have not chosen God and things spiritual as their life. *Exp. of the B.*

"The grave is the robing room for life eternal."

We see only the dark side of death, faith has eyes to see the other side which is full of light and glory for us who believe.

So little is this doctrine a hindrance to an active life in good works that it really forms its true basis. Only blind unbelief will accuse us of thinking only of the hereafter and forgetting to make this life what it should be. The fact is that none but they whose conversation is in heaven truly make this present life one of service, helpfulness, and elevation for

1 Cor. 15, 42b-49. 203

themselves and their fellow men. Paul himself is proof sufficient. Comp. verse 58!

St. Paul a Mighty Apostle of Christian Hope.

I. *He knows indeed that here we bear the image of the earthy.*
   1) Adam's creation of the dust of the earth.
   2) Our earthly life in the body.
   3) Its sad close when this corruptible body is laid away in the grave.

II. *But his heart embraces in faith the risen Christ as a life-giving spirit.*
   1) The second Adam in the glory of heaven.
   2) A life-giving spirit for us.
   3) Christ's life in Paul and us by faith.

III. *And thus he mightily proclaims that we shall at last bear the image of the heavenly.*
   1) These our earthly bodies shall rise from the dust.
   2) They shall be made like unto Christ's glorious body.
   3) They shall appear in incorruption, glory, power, as spiritual bodies.

"Jesus, my Redeemer, lives!" — the grand resurrection hymn of Princess Louise Henrietta. Beside this the shallow songs of others, such as "Beautiful Somewhere," "Lead, kindly light," etc., without even the name of Christ in them, or any clear statement of the resurrection of the body, fade into insignificance. The last couplet may summarize the message of our text:

"Fix your Heart beyond the Skies, Whither ye yourselves would Rise."

I. *Fix your hearts in faith on Christ who has gone before.*
   1) "Jesus, my Redeemer, lives,
      Christ, my Trust, is dead no more."

2) "In the strength this knowledge gives,
Shall not all my fears be o'er?"
3) "Calm, though death's long night be fraught
Still with many an anxious thought."
(This last line should end with a period, not with a question mark.)

II. *Fix your heart in hope that we shall follow him.*
1) "I shall see him with these eyes —
Him whom I shall surely know."
2) "Not another shall I rise;
With his love this heart shall glow."
3) "Only, there shall disappear
Weakness in and round me here."

Some venture to expect an immortality of the soul, and no more. They hope without an eternal rock to rest their hope on. They use their poor imagination, instead of Christ's blessed revelation.

St. Paul's Confession of Hope: "I Believe in the Resurrection of the Body."

He confesses:

I. *It is the body that shall rise again.*
II. *It is the risen Christ who shall raise it again.*
III. *It will be a glorious body when risen again.*

"On Jordan's stormy banks I stand,
And cast a wishful eye
To Canaan's fair and happy land,
Where my possessions lie."

With St. Paul on Jordan's Stormy Banks.

I. *The dark flood of death.*
II. *The mighty Lord who shall carry us across.*
III. *The fair possessions that lie beyond.*

1 Cor. 15, 42b-49.

Paul and the Two Adams.

I. *What Paul tells us of the first.*
   1) Adam, made of dust, fallen in sin.
   2) Adam's earthly children, sinners like him, and sown in corruption, *etc.*

II. *What Paul tells us of the second.*
   1) The Son of God, our Redeemer, a life-giving spirit.
   2) The second Adam's children, risen from sin, and to be raised in incorruption, *etc.*

IN CHAINS.
Acts 26, 22-30.

No picture of St. Paul is complete which fails to show us the apostle in chains. Several chapters in the Acts are devoted to this important portion of his life, and we find various references to it in the Epistles. Very suddenly the free activity of Paul came to an end, and instead of traveling from place to place and preaching the Gospel in the Gentile world in one center after another, returning from time to time to strengthen the churches he had established, he languished in confinement, fettered by a chain to his guard, and the days of weary waiting grew to months and even years. Felix put off the final decision of his case, then Festus also hesitated. Two years had passed, when Paul finally used his right as a Roman citizen and appealed his case directly to the emperor's tribunal at Rome. This meant a long and trying journey to the capital of the empire and the added delay incident to bringing his case at last before the busy emperor himself. During all this time Paul was a martyr in bonds.

There were three kinds of custody for Roman prisoners. One was the *custodia publica*, namely confinement in a public jail, generally a dungeon of the worst description, with the prisoner chained, perhaps even in a position of torture. The second was the *custodia libera;* the accused person was committed to the charge of a magistrate or senator, who became responsible for his appearance at trial. Only persons of the highest rank were committed to this very mild form of custody. The third was the *custodia militaris,* introduced at the time of the emperors. The accused was committed to the charge of a soldier, who became responsible with his own life for the safe keeping of the prisoner. One or two chains fastened the keeper and the prisoner together; sometimes both remained in the barracks, at other times the prisoner was allowed to stay with his guard in his own house. In Paul's case the third mode of confinement was used, and it seems that while he was in Cæsarea he was kept in the barracks; here he was treated with "indulgence," his friends being allowed to minister unto him, Felix hoping to be offered a bribe for his release. Acts 24, 23 and 27. While in Rome Paul was allowed to stay in his own rented house, Acts 28, 30; but here too the time of his imprisonment lengthened to two whole years.

We have chosen for our text a part of the dramatic account of Paul's appearance before Porcius Festus, King Herod Agrippa II., king of Chalcis, and his sister Bernice. We have thus the close of the apostle's address on this occasion, in which he sums up in a brief, compact statement his whole work and the Gospel he preached; and makes a telling appeal to his auditors. The climax is in verse 29, where he lifts up or stretches forward his fettered arm in a significant gesture and mentions "these bonds." It is surely an impressive picture of the apostle in chains, and the pericope includes the Gospel itself for which he gladly suffered these chains.

(26, 22) **Having therefore obtained the help that is**

from God, I stand unto this day testifying both to small and great, saying nothing but what the prophets and Moses did say should come; (23) **how that the Christ must suffer,** *and* **how that he first by the resurrection of the dead should proclaim light both to the people and to the Gentiles.**

When the scene had been staged in the governor's hall and Paul had received permission to speak, he "stretched forth his hand and made his defense." This consisted of an account of his conversion fitted in a masterly way to the occasion; it laid special emphasis on his call to be a witness of the divine Lord and Savior who had appeared to him, in order to turn Israel and the Gentiles from darkness to light, and from the power of Satan to God, so that they might receive remission of sins and an inheritance among them that are sanctified by faith in Christ. This call Paul declared he had followed in proper obedience, preaching everywhere that men should repent, turn to God, and do works worthy of repentance. For this — and for this alone — the apostle says he had been seized by the Jews, who then had attempted to kill him. Of the unjust treatment he had received at the hands of Felix, and of the attitude of Festus regarding his case, he says nothing. He summarizes only his own unwavering and courageous obedience to the Lord during all this time and up to the present moment.

Paul had preached "that they (Jews and Gentiles) should repent and turn to God, doing works worthy of repentance." On this account, ἕνεκα τούτων, the Jews had sought his life, endeavoring to stifle his voice. They had not succeeded, he still continued to bear this same witness, although during these past two years in bonds. The οὖν connects the murderous attempts of the Jews with his present situation and adds the sufficient explanation: **having obtained the help that is from God.** Ἐπικουρία is help in the sense of aid offered by an ally who hastens to give support. With all his foes thirsting for his blood the apostle did not stand alone, he had an ally stronger than all his foes. Τυγχάνειν is to meet, and thus to obtain; in all that befell the apostle God's help was present, so that he was able to lean upon it. And this was succor ἀπὸ τοῦ θεοῦ, from the Almighty himself, who knows how to rule even in the midst of his enemies. In one way Paul might have complained bitterly of the injustice of the Roman authorities; he does something better and greater, he comforts his heart with the thought of the divine providence that was clearly manifest in his bondage. God was keeping him and permitting him to go on bearing witness — even as at this moment before these dignitaries, — and his enemies could not hinder it. — **Unto this day** refers to the special opportunity granted to Paul just now in having this audience before him; at the same time it recalls all the gracious manifestations that had continued so long, from the first moment of his capture on. And God who had been his ally thus far surely could not forsake him in the future. In any hard and difficult trial which God sends us it is a comforting thing to stop and count our mercies up to the present hour or day, though the trial itself be not yet finished. — There is a note of victory in ἕστηκα, **I stand,** the perfect in the present sense: I have stood and thus still stand; Meyer: *ich halte Stand*. Nothing has been able to move or overthrow him; but the credit for this belongs wholly to his divine helper — Μαρτυρόμενος (from the deponent verb μαρτύρομαι), **testifying,** refers back to μάρτυς in verse 16: witnessing, attesting, and thus assuring. Meyer defends the reading μαρτυρούμενος (from μαρτυρέω), which would be passive: "attested," the following datives then being the agents: "by small and great." The trouble with this reading is that it is not true to the facts in the case, since the Jews denounced Paul instead of giving him the testimony that he was in accord with the prophets and Moses. The present participle has the sense: continuing to testify; the apostle never desisted, no danger or fear hushed his testimony at any time. To testify is to speak of one's own experience or personal knowledge. The apostolic testimony is authoritative for all time; but we who accept this testimony are ourselves to experience its saving power, so that all true Gospel preaching is still to be a personal testimony on the part of the preacher, and likewise a personal testimony on the part of confessing believers. — **Both to small and great,** comp. 8, 10, can hardly mean "young and old" (Meyer), but: "both to men of low and of high estate." All along in his captivity Paul had to do with these two classes, and never with children. Even now a common soldier was at his side, and there were other guards and attendants; and at the same time there were the governor, the king, and his sister. Paul had the same Gospel for his judges and for their servants; he knew nothing of the modern folly of accommodating the foolishness of preaching to men of science and modern education. They are all nothing but miserable sinners, and only the grace of God in Christ Jesus can save them through repentance and faith. — Paul now gives a summary statement of his testimony: **saying nothing but what the prophets and Moses did say should come.** He puts οὐδὲν ἐκτός emphatically forward; λέγων is continuous, like μαρτυρόμενος, testifying and saying ever and always. The adverb ἐκτός governs the genitive, and ὧν = τούτων ἅ, the indefinite antecedent and its relative drawn into one, using the case of the former; μελλόντων thus also appears in the genitive, instead of the accusative. The prophets are here mentioned first, but the sentence is so constructed as to give Moses the most emphatic place: "saying nothing but what both the prophets did say should come, and Moses" — because the Jews had accused Paul especially of teaching people to forsake Moses, Acts 21, 21. The aorist ἐλάλησαν is historical, and γίνεσθαι preserves the present tense of the direct discourse. The things about to come, τὰ μέλλοντα, are those that refer to the Messiah and his kingdom of grace and of glory. Some of these had come: redemption, the outpouring of the Spirit, the establishment of a new covenant and a new covenant people. Others, such as the final judgment, were yet to come. Paul here gives his hearers the solemn assurance that in all his preaching and teaching he has not gone beyond what the Old Testament teaches and the Jews themselves professed to believe. He puts the seal of verity upon the Old Test., and he uses that Test. as a seal of verity for his own teaching. Besser rightly says: "Thus the prophetic word becomes new in the apostolic, and the entire apostolic word is old in the prophetic." Of course, the one is promise, the other fulfillment, but this is the very point on which their essential identity rests.

(23) **How that Christ must suffer,** is really in the problematic form εἰ παθητὸς ὁ χριστός, "whether Christ must suffer," note the margin. But Robertson (p. 1024) rightly states that in this protasis the apodosis is really contained, so that εἰ amounts to ὅτι. The sense then is: whether he must suffer as the prophets and Moses say that he must. The question which Paul always debated with the Jews was, whether the Messiah must suffer; and he asserted that the prophets and Moses taught that he must. Luther: *ob Christus sollte leiden*. The actual sense is best given by the R. V.: "how that" *etc*. The verbal adjective παθητός = subject to suffering, liable to suffering; but as Meyer rightly adds: *passibilis*, not in the sense of capability but in the sense of divine determination or ordination. Hence the word has the sense here of "must suffer," *necessati patiendi obnoxius*. The suffering of the Messiah was contrary to all the Jewish ideas concerning him; they would not accept this interpretation of the prophecies, and hence scorned the crucified Christ. He was an offense to them, because they had planned for themselves a Messiah who should do nothing but conquer and triumph in outward victory over his enemies. — *And* **how he first by the resurrection of the dead should proclaim light both to the people and to the Gentiles.** This is added without the connecting "and" in Greek, making the statement more lively. Πρῶτος like παθητός is put forward for emphasis, both are predicative: "that he as the first" *etc*. But ἐξ ἀναστάσεως is not in-

strumental, as the R. V. has it: *"by* the resurrection"; it does not modify μέλλει καταγγέλειν, but πρῶτος: *als Erster aus der Totenauferweckung.* Stier is right: πρῶτος ἐξ ἀναστάσεως νεκρῶν is equivalent in meaning to πρῶτος ἀναστὰς ἐκ νεκρῶν, the First-risen from the dead = the First-born from the dead, Col. 1, 18. This connects immediately with παθητός, the suffering and death of the Messiah. The prophets and Moses foretold both, the two in connection with each other; and Paul taught the same as regards the fulfillment effected in Christ. But the Jewish rejection of a suffering Messiah blinded their eyes, so that they failed to believe his resurrection from the dead. — This second member, however, contains two main thoughts compounded into one, namely the resurrection from the dead, and the proclamation of light: as the risen Savior he would proclaim light. Stier: "According to prophecy, as understood by the apostolic spirit, from the resurrection of Christ results the light promised for all the world, the light of God, to which all the Gentiles were to turn, leaving behind them the darkness of Satan. In this expression Paul combines the first 'opening of the eyes' with the 'last inheritance of the saints in light': here, too, 'the life is the light of men'; and in him, the Son, is this life for all, John 1, 4. . . . Of the 'light to lighten the Gentiles' Simeon had already spoken, Luke 2, 32; comp. Acts 13, 47. Christ himself shows the light, by causing it to be shown by his messengers through his Spirit." Paul here had before him a Jew in Agrippa and a Gentile in Festus; the appeal of his Gospel went out to both. In combining "the people and the Gentiles" the apostle, like the prophets of old, viewed the kingdom of the Messiah as world-wide, "a kingdom of sanctification and resurrection through faith in Jesus." All this Paul could say because of the power of Christ's death and resurrection, conquering sin, death, hell, and every foe. He was the first to break the bonds of death, rising not like Lazarus to this earthly life, but to the life eternal, and not by the power of another merely, but by his own power — he by his own hand opening the gates of death and leaving them open behind him for us all. In μέλλει the tense of the direct discourse is preserved; also the two sentences with εἰ must be read as following ἐλάλησεν, not as following λέγων, for these were the things the prophets said would come (μελλόντων, taken up again by μέλλει).

(24) **And as he thus made his defense, Festus said with a loud voice, Paul, thou art mad; thy much learning doth turn thee to madness.** (25) **But Paul saith, I am not mad, most excellent Festus; but speak forth words of truth and soberness.** (26) **For the king knoweth of these things, unto whom also I speak freely: for I am persuaded that none of these things is hidden from him; for this hath not been done in a corner.**

The present tense ἀπολογουμένου shows that what Paul was now speaking caused Festus to make his exclamation. He probably had listened with interest at first, expecting to hear something that might serve him in writing to the emperor to whom he had to send Paul. But the longer Paul spoke, the less hope there was for this, and the more strange his words seemed to this Roman, who evidently had not read the Greek Old Testament, and lacked all feeling and un-

Acts 26, 22-30. 215

derstanding for what the apostle here presented. Finally he bursts out with: Μαίνῃ, Παῦλε. He utters this **with a loud voice,** which betrays his feeling. He is provoked at the apostle. Bengel writes: *Videbat Festus, naturam non agere in Paulo; sed gratiam non vidit.* — The addition: **thy much learning,** *etc.,* is not a softening of the first exclamation, but a substantiation of it. By γράμματα books can hardly be meant, but rather the things that one finds in them, learning, *etc.* Jacobus writes: "The great doctrines of Christianity seem to the mere worldling like jargon, and the earnest enforcement of them, like insanity." And Lindhammer: "The world considers others sane as long as they rave, and raving, when they cease to rave and become sane. As long as Paul was exceedingly mad (verse 11) and raved, he passed for a bright fellow; but when he knew that he had been raving and became a Christian, they thought him mad. But the turn will come, when the wordly will say of the righteous: We fools thought their life foolish, and now they are counted among the children of God."

(25) Without being ruffled in the least Paul answers the governor. His reply shows that he understood Festus to mean that he was indeed crazy. He does not use "a loud voice" like the governor, for no foolish feeling carries him into heat. He uses the respectful address, κράτιστε Φῆστε. He refutes the governor's apparent proof, based only on what the governor surmised, by directing his attention to what he had just heard from him: ἀληθείας καὶ σωφροσύνης ῥήματα, utterances such as belong to and characterize **truth,** real facts, actual happenings, and spiritual realities; utterances such as pertain to and mark also **sober-**

ness, or as Jacobus calls it: "sound-mindedness," moderation, good sense, self-control. "Truth" is objective; "soberness" subjective. Paul was speaking of realities and verities, not of fancies, dreams, speculations; and he was speaking of these sensibly, with good judgment, not with exaggeration, fanciful distortion, impossible additions of nonsense. Luke alone uses the verb ἀποφθέγγεσθαι (comp. 4, 2), to speak forth clearly and loudly; it is a choice word, used by the LXX of prophesying, and by later Greek writers of oracles. It fits well the dignified, clear, and plain statement Paul had made on this occasion.

(26) The γάρ offers proof for Paul's claim to truth and soberness of utterance. **The king knoweth of these things,** namely of the *facts* concerning Jesus' death and resurrection and the Christian church that resulted. He must have known all the outward things connected with Jesus, especially also his miracles. The implication is that Festus, who heard of these things for the first time and found them strange and new, was not justified in thinking them merely the inventions of an unbalanced mind. — The addition: πρὸς ὃν παρρησιαζόμενος λαλῶ, indicates that the apostle had Agrippa especially in mind when he made his appeal, whom also he had repeatedly addressed in his speech. The participle conveys the thought that before the king Paul spoke **freely,** openly, holding back nothing, since the king was conversant with these things and would understand. Agrippa was fully acquainted with Jewish affairs and with the Jewish Scriptures, and as a guardian of the temple he had the official duty to busy himself with these matters. — So Paul adds: **for I am persuaded that none of these**

Acts 26, 22-30.

things is hidden from him. The emphatic positions in the sentence are occupied by λανθάνειν and by οὐθέν, which according to Robertson goes with this infinitive although placed after πείθομαι, p. 1094: "there has escaped from him of these things, I am persuaded, not a thing"; really with the double negative: "not persuaded, not a thing," making the negation the more emphatic. Even in this statement Paul is careful and sober, he voices only his own conviction, and then at once justifies himself even for having this: **for this hath not been done in a corner.** Agrippa could hardly have helped knowing all about it. The τούτων of the previous clauses is now compressed into the singular τοῦτο = this great thing concerning Jesus Christ. "Not in a corner" = publicly, in the very capital of the nation, with the Sanhedrim and the governor himself involved, and Jesus a national figure, whose fame had filled the land. Thus soberly and patiently Paul sets the governor right. At the same time he does two other things: he maintains the greatness and importance of the cause for which he stands — it is not an obscure little affair that nobody knows anything about; and he paves the way, by addressing the governor regarding the personal knowledge of the king, for a direct personal appeal to the king. For though Paul is in chains, a poor prisoner receiving the most unjust treatment at the hands of the proud Roman law, he is the master on this notable occasion, as on others like it. His message and his personality place him in this dominating position. And he always uses it, as Christ did even more before him, not for any personal ends merely, here only to defend and **justify himself,** and if possible gain his release, but to do his work as an apostle, to preach the Gospel to the poor sinners before him who needed it so sadly. Whether he stood before the aristocracy of learning as at Athens, or before the aristocracy of power as here in Festus' hall, he had but one grand aim, and he kept true to that.

(27) **King Agrippa, believest thou the prophets? I know that thou believest.** (28) **And Agrippa** *said* **unto Paul, With but little persuasion thou wouldest fain make me a Christian.** (29) **And Paul** *said,* **I would to God, that whether with little or with much, not thou only but also all that hear me this day, might become such as I am, except these bonds.**

Here this great prisoner's great purpose is fully expressed; his παρρησία leaves nothing to be desired. Though a prisoner he fears not to ask of a king a question pertaining to that king's own immortal soul. The apostle had spoken of the prophets and Moses, verse 22; for a Jew these were to be the gateway to Christ. So he does not ask: Believest thou in Christ? but: "Believest thou the prophets?" A hearty yea to this question would lead to a presentation of the prophecies by which the prophets set forth the things concerning Christ. And so faith in the prophets would turn to faith in Christ. Paul was leading Agrippa to take the first decisive step. — When he adds: οἶδα ὅτι πιστεύεις, he in a way preempts Agrippa's answer, but only in a way creditable to Agrippa himself as an honest Jew, and to the apostle himself in so thinking of Agrippa. We must not lay too much into πιστεύεις; it is used with the dative τοῖς προφήταις, and means to believe that what the prophets had spoken is truth, fact, not fancies or lies. It is *assent* to their words that Paul presumes on the part of Agrippa, and this he had a right to presume until Agrippa himself should repudiate the prophets. — (28) It is difficult to say what reply Paul expected from the king. It may have been some plain word of assent to the words of the prophets. The reply he did receive is of a different kind. Agrippa sees the goal toward which the apostle would lead him, namely Christian faith, and thus reaches forward far beyond the question itself as put to him: **With but little persuasion thou wouldest fain make me a Christian.** The grammarian Robertson calls this sentence, from his standpoint, a hard one. Quite a chapter might be written on the history of its interpretation. Robertson asks: "Is $\mu\epsilon$ the object of $\pi\epsilon\iota\theta\epsilon\iota\varsigma$ or of $\pi o\iota\tilde{\eta}\sigma a\iota$? Can $\pi\epsilon\iota\theta\epsilon\iota\varsigma$ be 'try by persuasion'?" We restrict ourselves to the following statements. Paul's answer $\epsilon\nu$ $\dot{o}\lambda\iota\gamma\omega$ $\kappa a\iota$ $\epsilon\nu$ $\mu\epsilon\gamma\dot{a}\lambda\omega$ helps to determine the sense of Agrippa's $\dot{\epsilon}\nu$ $\dot{o}\lambda\iota\gamma\omega$, for it seems out of the question to take the one expression in one sense and the other in another. Stier defends $\dot{\epsilon}\nu$ $\pi o\lambda\lambda\tilde{\omega}$ for $\dot{\epsilon}\nu$ $\mu\epsilon\gamma\dot{a}\lambda\omega$ and holds to the meaning "almost" for $\dot{\epsilon}\nu$ $\dot{o}\lambda\iota\gamma\omega$. The codices are against him on the reading, and that about settles the other point. But we think Stier is right over against quite a few prominent commentators in refusing to take Agrippa's reply as a sneer. Even Besser calls it *das leichte Scherzwort*. Stier writes: "Are we justified in giving the apostle credit for so little apostolic acuteness, that he should mistake a mocker for one inclined to believe, with whom perhaps some good might be done? Would we ascribe to Paul so much common, weak good-nature that after this manifest ridicule he should reply to Agrippa in a friendly way, just as if he were in earnest?" Stier's observations are decidedly to the point. There is no real reason for taking Agrippa's words as a scoff, *Spott* (Meyer), "spoken ironically and in contempt" (Conybeare, Schaeffer), *etc.* The words were uttered soberly, not contemptuously. Ἐν ὀλίγῳ cannot mean "almost," A. V., for this would be ὀλίγου or some other form; the revival hymn, "Almost persuaded," loses this scriptural allusion. Nor will it do to supply χρόνῳ, on account of Paul's answer, in which ἐν μεγάλῳ cannot be combined with χρόνῳ. The neuter ὀλίγῳ is substantized; in Eph. 3, 3 ἐν ὀλίγῳ means "summarily." So here. Jacobus has a good explanation: "Agrippa feels himself hard pressed by Paul's arguments, and finds that he is in a sort held by his faith in Judaism to admit Christianity. He cannot deny his religion — he is not prepared to admit these inferences from his belief in the prophets. Festus scoffs and Paul insists, and Agrippa thus suddenly thrust into a dilemma, can do nothing but protest against being drawn so *summarily* into an admission of the Christian system. He sees where all this close pressure of Paul's argument is carrying him, and he cries out, You are summarily persuading me (attempting to persuade me) to become a Christian. As though he had said, You are crowding me to this conclusion, which I am not yet prepared to accept. Paul was thus shutting him up to the faith, as if in spite of himself, and in a sort compelling him to embrace the Christian faith, as a necessary consequence of Judaism and as the proper fulfillment of the prophets. And just at this point, where he ought to have believed, but would not, he can get no relief except by dismissing the subject.

Agrippa sees that Paul is aiming at the practical end of converting his hearers to Christianity, and he feels the striking appropriateness and force of his positions." Robertson, p. 880, lists πείθεις as an example of the inchoative or conative present, in this case where an act has been begun but interrupted. So the translation of the R. V. gives Agrippa's words correctly: "With but little persuasion thou wouldest fain make me a Christian." It may be noted also that Agrippa uses Χριστιανόν, comp. Acts 11, 26, which was of Gentile origin and milder and less abusive than the Jewish designation "Nazarene." To say that it was pronounced contemptuously (Lechler) is gratuitous. Agrippa declined to become a Christian; we would not expect him to use an honor name for Christ's followers, it is quite enough that he used the name he did use.

(29) Paul's reply is masterly from the point of the situation in which it was made; at the same time it reveals all the nobility and love in his heart. Εὐξαίμην ἂν τῷ θεῷ, the potential optative in an apodosis with the protasis unexpressed: **I would to God,** or literally: "I would pray to God," if *etc.* — with whatever one may care to supply. The expression betrays deep feeling. — In ἐν ὀλίγῳ Paul repeats Agrippa's word, but he adds the strong counterpart ἐν μεγάλῳ, which shows that χρόνῳ cannot be supplied. **Whether with little or with much** really needs no addition, the neuter adjectives being used as nouns; we may say with Vincent: "with little or with great pains," effort, work, or whatever we care, as long as we remember that the added noun is put in place only of the indefinite "something." — The balanced thought thus

introduced receives a companion: **not thou only, but also all that hear me this day** — whether for one it require little or for another much. While Paul had addressed his words to the king in a personal manner, he here declares that his heart went out to all assembled that day within range of his voice. Some of these might indeed pity him in his bondage; Paul sees that their spiritual bondage is a thousand times worse than his which was only bodily. Did he think, perhaps, of what the grace of God had done for him on the road to Damascus? It was ἐν μεγάλῳ that he had been brought to Christ, and the arm of God's grace had not been shortened — think of the victories it had already achieved through Paul! — And this is the wish that he would like to put into the form of a prayer: that they **might become such as I am, except these bonds,** γενέσθαι, 2nd aorist, pointing to a single act, which here would be conversion; comp. τοῦ ἐπιστρέψαι κτλ. in verse 18. It is difficult to see how this aorist could be combined with καὶ ἐν ὀλίγῳ καὶ ἐν μεγάλῳ in the sense of "in all respects," which the American Committee would place in the margin. Might become (by conversion, in one act) "in all respects" like Paul, is out of the question, for conversion would make them like him only in one respect, of course, in the essential one. And this is what Paul's heart desires. — Perhaps he stretched forth his fettered arm when he added dramatically: παρεκτὸς τῶν δεσμῶν τούτων. His bonds were an honor to him. and the Lord made their weight light for him; but the apostle's magnanimous heart would spare others the severe trial of having to bear similar burdens. "This Christian magnanimity, wishing those who unjustly confined him nothing but good, wishing them everything but evil — is a splendid specimen of the true Christian spirit even in chains. So able to give a reason for his hope — so bold, calm, and convincing in his defense of the truth — so earnest and tender in enforcing it, and yearning so at heart for the salvation of his persecutors, Paul wins a glorious victory. And this last and fullest vindication of the Christian cause in the face of Jewish and Gentile dignitaries, before he quits the Holy Land for the metropolis of the heathen world, will stand on record wherever the Gospel is preached (like Mary's anointing), as a memorial of him." Jacobus.

(30) **And the king rose up, and the governor, and Bernice, and they that sat with them.**

The audience was at an end. Agrippa himself ended it by rising to leave. The meeting had been arranged at his request, Acts 25, 22, and thus he was privileged to prolong or to shorten it, the governor politely deferring to him. But Agrippa had felt Paul's touch upon his heart, and from this strange and unexpected power he withdrew. Alas, his hour of grace had come, and when he drew away he left salvation behind him. How many there are like him along the road which the Gospel has traveled! According to rank the others also arose and filed out of the hall in state. The servants bowed as they passed. Through another door the guards led Paul out. No servants bowed in deference before this royal man, for he wore a chain not of gold upon his arm. But all the glory of the world is as nothing before the noble Christian faith, fortitude, and love of this God's holy apostle — though in chains.

HOMILETICAL HINTS.

The material in this text is of the very finest. Here is a strong, compact summary of the Gospel; a noble believer and confessor who puts the Gospel into action; and here are proud, obdurate sinners, and we hear the impact of the Gospel power upon their souls. It is above all St. Paul who here rivets our attention. His long imprisonment has not altered him. He may be pale and emaciated from long confinement, but the holy flame burns with undimmed brightness and energy in his soul. He is sterling all through. The chain that fetters him only helps to set his nobility of soul into bolder relief. The fires of tribulation have done nothing but make his faith shine with greater intensity and power.

When a preacher receives the gift of wielding the sword of the Word with ability, the world is not unwilling to concede that, to a certain extent, he does possess talent, but alleges that he preaches the Gospel only for the purpose of displaying his skill. And yet, we are surely not actors; and as little is it madness, when in the name of the living God we speak of eternity, of a Savior, or of the resurrection. Such words are rational and true, and are supported by the eternal truth of God; and nothing more unequivocally demonstrates their truth than precisely the opposition of the human heart. — A childlike and simple faith in the whole revealed truth of the Scriptures is represented as belonging to the narrow-mindedness of the old times; the doctrine of justification by faith in the merits of Christ is called a pagan, sanguinary theology, *etc.* When one begins to occupy himself earnestly and seriously with the duties of religion, and breaks the ties which had bound him to the world, he is pitied as a man whom religious melancholy has betrayed into extravagances, and whose mind has become affected by the excessive study of the Bible. (Thoughts of Gerok, *Apostelgeschichte,* elaborated by Schaeffer in Commentary of Lange.)

The continuance of our life could be no real benefit and joy, if it were devoted to any other purpose than that of diligently serving our Savior.

Agrippa's father when he lay dying in Cæsarea consoled

himself with the reflection that though his career was prematurely cut short, yet at any rate he had led a splendid life. And such as the parent had been, such were the children.

Amid the hard labor of politics, in the merciless war for mine and thine, for honor, gold, and enjoyment, there had died in the heart of this Roman the feeling for any but this poor earthly world. This is the soil in which in all ages the wisdom of the five senses flourishes: whatever we cannot see and grasp, does not exist, at least is without value, is fancy. To devote one's life to something that cannot be seen, cannot be put into figures, or transmuted into pleasure; to follow the promptings and powers of an invisible world, and to expect of men that they are to seek their salvation and peace in these things: this is just as hard for the natural mind to understand to-day, as it was long ago; it is an offense, a thing from which to turn away. And this explains how to-day some incline even to deny the personal honesty of Paul, which Festus still admitted, and as a rule attribute only the most hateful motives to views like his. Dryander.

Brenz often preached to empty benches. After one of his services a stranger walked home with him and expressed his surprise that so few people had attended. They came past the town well in the market-place, and Brenz asked whether the stranger knew what was the finest thing about this well. He asked what it was. This, said Brenz, that it tirelessly gives its water whether people come and get it or not. And this is the finest quality of a true evangelical preacher, that he sends forth the water of life ceaselessly, whether the world cares to hear him or not. Gerok.

Those are the true court preachers, who are not deterred by the star *on* the breast of the prince, from inquiring whether the heavenly morning star is also shining *in* the breast.

Agrippa: The heart was touched, the mind convinced, the conscience aroused, the hour favorable, namely the hour of grace which might decide for our eternal welfare — but something was lacking. What? A bar that we refused to let the Holy Ghost remove; a hardness that we would not let him melt away; a love of the world and of sin that we would not let him break. And so the hour passed, the opportunity was gone.

We were not saved; in fact, having missed the golden moment, we were farther away from salvation than ever.

Gerok has this picture: There he stands, the man of God in his chains, mocked of Festus, politely turned off by Agrippa, disappointed in his joyful hope of striking success for his preaching, and yet firm in his faith, full of assurance in God, his heart not cooled in the least as to its love for the souls before him, and as to its zeal to win hearts for his Lord.

Dryander exposes Agrippa's heart: Although still a man of youthful age, he was a voluptuary, an adulterer. But nothing so surely prevents admission to God, so positively excludes from understanding religious truth, as the depravity which caters to the appetites, the cultus of the flesh. This is beyond question: the world of faith is a world of things pure, chaste, holy, true. And it is equally beyond question: he who gives reins to the flesh, loses himself in a world of things impure, dishonest, lying, in which nothing pure and holy can continue to exist. This is the double reason why the apostle's powerful appeal to Agrippa received the answer it did. — And he portrays the apostle: Stoned in Lystra, scourged in Philippi, mocked in Athens, almost torn to pieces by the populace in Ephesus, imprisoned in Jerusalem, the traces of his two years of confinement upon his features and the chains upon his hands, he stands nevertheless before the governor and the king with an inner clearness and greatness in his soul, which could not but affect those who beheld him. It is a realization of those glorious words, which he wrote to the Corinthians (2 Cor. 6, 9, *etc.*) : "As dying, and, behold, we live; as chastened, and not killed; as sorrowful, yet always rejoicing; as poor, yet making many rich; as having nothing, and yet possessing all things." We indeed hear from his lips more than once, how the greatness of his mission, to be a steward of the mysteries of God (1 Cor. 4, 1), almost pressed him to the ground. The request of the Old Testament prophets, who wanted to withdraw from the load of their task, with their cry: "Lord, send, whom thou wilt," is not unknown to him. But at the same time he knows, that though he is not sufficient of himself, God has made him sufficient to bear the office of the new covenant (2 Cor. 3, 6). He knows that in his office he possesses something that lifts him up and beyond the entire world, that a message is entrusted to him by which he, though poor, may make even a Festus and an Agrippa rich, he, though a prisoner, may set free these captives of unbelief and sin. Though he be the only one to stand for the truth — the truth itself will for this reason not be less. And it alone is the final power to which the victory belongs. And truth needs no other weapon than the testimony which he gives it. A king of truth the Lord himself had called himself before Pilate, and thereby cast a terror into the Roman's soul. And where but one ray of the truth of Jesus Christ is embodied in a man, there he too possesses a similar impress of royal highness. And this is what meets us in Paul. And we see it shining again and again in the countless witnesses of truth who have become his successors. This may help to make us fearless against the resistance which to-day opposes the testimony of the truth. It bears its power within itself and has its allies in the consciences of men (2 Cor. 4, 2). — But in his patience there is something still deeper. We have already learned to know it as the deepest secret and the real moving power of the personality of Paul, the power of every personality to whom the office of caring for souls has been committed — it is called the earnestness of *priestly love*. As a prisoner who pleaded for his liberty Paul stood before his judges. But the thought of defense, the burning desire for liberation has been swallowed up for him in the greater thought, to plead that his judges may be brought into the captivity of his Master, Christ. It is with this priestly love that he feels deep grief for those who withdraw themselves from his words (Rom. 9, 2), and maternal joy, when he is able to bring the erring to faith (Gal. 4, 19). With this love he once more knocks at the hearts of his hearers and calls to the corrupt Agrippa: "I would to God, that not only thou," *etc*. This love is the continuation of the love with which the Lord himself, refused by his nation, rejected, condemned, still loves on, ceases not until nailed to the cross, to turn souls unto the way of salvation, even though they be condemned malefactors. Human love, even the noblest, is very temporal, seeks only things human. This priestly love, ripened in the school of Christ, bears an eternal power in it. And God be praised — it has not died in the church of Christ.

Our text has been used quite rarely, hence there is a dearth of outlines that might prove suggestive.

St. Paul — a Victor in Chains.

I. *Even in chains he preaches a victorious Lord.*
II. *Even in chains he proclaims a victorious Gospel.*
III. *Even in chains he confesses a victorious faith.*
IV. *Even in chains he manifests a victorious love.*

Paul and his Noble Auditors: How Men Treat the Truth of the Gospel.

I. *Men like Festus reject it entirely.*
II. *Men like Agrippa turn to it at most only in part.*
III. *Men like Paul give to it their whole hearts and lives.*

Adapted from Gerok.

Chains did not Change the Great Apostle.

I. *They did not alter his Gospel.*
II. *They did not weaken his faith.*
III. *They did not dampen his passion for souls.*

St. Paul's Sad Experience with those who are Lost.

I. *His Gospel of salvation indeed attracts them.*
   1) It opens up an entirely new world for them — Paul's enthusiasm moves even the cold heart of Festus.
   2) It touches them with the powers of this new world — even Agrippa felt this touch as never before.

II. *Yet the Gospel of salvation eventually repels them.*
   1) Because they obstinately cling to their old perverted thoughts.
   2) Because they obdurately prefer the old evil of their wicked lives.

Thoughts from Lisco.

Acts 26, 22-30.

The Noblest Things in St. Paul's Soul.

I. *His unwavering faith.*
II. *His unceasing confession.*
III. *His unflinching courage.*
IV. *His undismayed love.*

Stronger than Iron Chains.

I. *The trust that bound Paul to Christ.*
II. *The love that joined him to his fellow men.*

FACING THE END.
2 Tim. 4, 16-18.

For the closing text of this brief series one might desire 2 Tim. 4, 6-8, and indeed no better choice could be made. But this pericope is often used for funeral occasions, and it also occurs in the Eisenach epistle selections, where the author has given it his exposition, which he naturally would not care to repeat here. We, accordingly, make another choice, a brief section from the same chapter, one that indeed lacks the beautiful imagery of the other text, but is nevertheless filled with the same deep feeling, which comes out in a burst of praise to God at the end. It is this doxology, uttered in the sure expectation of final condemnation before the Roman court, and execution to follow, that makes our text exceptionally fine for our purpose. It shows us, just like the other text, how Paul *faced the end*.

We would like to know much more than we do concerning the last years of the apostle's life. It is hazardous to make detailed conjectures, and best to be satisfied with a few positive points. It is quite certain that Paul was released from his first imprisonment and lived some five years longer. He probably carried out his desire to visit the churches in Asia, and it is quite certain that he also turned to the west and penetrated as far as Spain. Clemens Romanus writes: "before his martyrdom Paul went to *the extreme west*", and the Muratori Fragment names directly: *"Spain."* After this, it seems, he spent some time in Nicopolis, and it must have been either here, or, after a journey from here to Rome, in the capital itself that his arrest followed and the trial that ended with his execution. He had been released in the spring of the year 63. In the following year, July 18 to 24, while he was absent from Rome, the city was burned, a second conflagration occurring a few days after. Nero himself was accused of having caused the fire; but he and his partisans charged the Christians with this crime, causing some to be crucified, others to be arrayed in wild beasts' skins and hunted to death by dogs, and still others to be wrapped in pitch robes and set on fire at night to illuminate the Vatican circus and Nero's gardens, while that monster played the charioteer. The Christians were now clearly distinguished from the Jews. Just what the charge against Paul was on his second arrest we do not know; it seems to have been double or threefold, most probably that for one thing he had conspired with the Christians to burn Rome three or four years prior, and for another that he was introducing and upholding a novel and unlawful religion in the empire. This time Paul's imprisonment was much more severe, yet he was acquitted of the "first" charge, 2 Tim. 4, 17, though no patron dared to advocate his cause, or any defender come to his aid. He does not seem to have been confined in the Mamertine or Tullianum prison, but he certainly was under military custody, most likely in the barracks of the legionaries, where it was more difficult to reach him. His case was not tried by the emperor himself, but by the "rulers" (Clemens: ἐπὶ τῶν ἡγουμένων). The trial most likely took place in one of the two Pauline basilicæ, named after L. Æmil. Paulus, who built the one and restored the other. These were large halls, where hundreds could be present and hear. When the first charge came to trial Alexander the coppersmith appeared, either as an accuser or as a witness, against Paul and damaged his case greatly, although he failed in his ultimate object. The Second Epistle to Timothy was written immediately after this first trial, and Paul longs greatly to have Timothy hasten to his side. He is filled with the gravest fears regarding the second charge and his trial on that, and these fears were justified. Luke proved his faithful companion to the last. Nero was in Greece, and the final trial occurred, it seems, under his representative, Helius Cæsareanus, the freedman of Claudius, who was prefect of Rome and Italy. Dion Cassius says, that as Nero aped the minstrels, the freedman aped Nero. The best account declares that Paul was martyred on the Ostian way. It was probably to avoid the sympathy which his influence had excited that he was executed outside of the city by a military escort, with *the sword,* his Roman citizenship exempting him from torture and crucifixion. He sealed his faith with his blood in the last year of Nero's reign, who died June 9, 68.

The entire last chapter of our Epistle is written with the prospect of death vividly before the apostle's eyes. He urges Timothy: "Do thy diligence to come shortly unto me" — ere it be too late; and again: "Do thy diligence to come before winter." We do not know whether Timothy came in time of not — let us hope that he did. Paul briefly refers to the circumstances of his first trial.

(4, 16) **At my first defense no one took my part, but all forsook me: may it not be laid to their account.**

Paul tells Timothy of his sad experience, it seems to let him feel the more how much he needed his presence just now. Ἐν τῇ πρώτῃ μου ἀπολογίᾳ refers to the first defense Paul had made, at the first hearing of his case by the Roman court. The word "first" implies that at least one other hearing would follow. Some commentators speak of but one, others note that more than one hearing might follow. This **first defense,** to conclude from the last statement in verse 17, had been successful. Alexander the coppersmith had indeed "greatly withstood" Paul's "words," namely his speeches of defense before the court, but he had not succeeded. Just in what capacity this man had acted, and just who he was to act thus, is left to conjecture. But, as far as the text itself goes, this withstanding of Paul's λόγοι on the part of Alexander ought not to be referred to λόγοι uttered in preaching the Gospel to him, or anything of that sort, but to the λόγοι which represent Paul's ἀπολογία. The man must have been prompted by the most vicious and vindictive hate. To offset this base and desperate hostility at his trial Paul writes that no one appeared to take his part, that he was left utterly alone: οὐδείς μοι παρεγένετο. He even makes the statement emphatic by adding the negative: **but all forsook me,** ἀλλὰ πάντες με ἐγκατέλειπον (or 2nd aor., ἐγκατέλιπον). Some incline to take this in a general way, so that it refers to all of Paul's friends. They then, like Stellhorn, refer even to Luke, of whom Paul says in verse 11: "Only Luke is with me", **they add the reference to 2 Tim. 1, 7,** the idea that such a weakness might have been possible even in a man like Luke. It is of little use to argue mere possibilities in this case. The way Paul mentions Luke in verse 11, and speaks also of other of his friends and assistants, warrants us in concluding that here, in voicing his disappointment concerning "all" who abandoned him at his trial, none of these is meant. If Luke braved the danger of remaining faithfully at Paul's side during his rigorous confinement, and was even now at the apostle's side, it certainly does not look as if he had been unfaithful in the critical hour of the trial. Both the imperfect ἐγκατέλειπον, "continue to abandon," and the aorist ἐγκατέλιπον, "did abandon," read as if the πάντες of whom this is said abandoned the apostle altogether. How could Luke, or any other close friend and assistant of the apostle, have done such a thing and then right after it still be with Paul? The thing has a decidedly impossible look. So we conclude that πάντες must refer to others of whom Paul had a right to expect that they would rally to his special defense. Another question is whether those mentioned in verse 21 can be meant, Eubulus, Pudens, Linus, Claudia, and the brethren. This too looks altogether improbable. It is hard to assume, even with 1, 7 *etc.* in mind, that these dear friends abandoned the apostle and that then hard upon it he put down their names in his letter as joining with him in sending greetings to Timothy. Even of these people long dead and gone we would

not care to assume evil, when there is really *no*
evidence at hand, nothing but surmise, that they are
in the least guilty. By παρεγένετο we most safely
understand an assistance that would count at a trial
at court. Such assistance could be rendered only
by people who were in a position to appear as material witnesses, or, as the Roman court procedure
of the day allowed, who could appear in the capacity
of *patroni et amici,* or possibly as legal *procuratores.*
Conybeare writes of Paul's position at this time: "No
advocate would venture to plead his cause, no *procura-
tor* to aid him in arranging the evidence, no *patronus*
(such as he might have found, perhaps, in the powerful Æmilian house) to appear as his supporter, and
to deprecate, according to ancient usage, the severity
of the sentence." A far better reference here, than
1, 17 *etc.* as it might refer to people named in this
Epistle, is 1, 15; Paul may have counted on powerful intercessors from Asia Minor, or on others especially qualified in Rome. Nor is it necessary here
to think only of Christians, for he had other very
influential friends, and Christians, however zealous
for Paul, by their very religious profession may have
been barred out altogether. In fact, we know that
Paul, though he was acquitted at first, was condemned
later, and there is but one charge, as far as any fair
surmise goes, that could have proved fatal in this
way, namely that of establishing an illicit religion. If
anything is fair, it seems that this charge handicapped
all Paul's Christian friends at his trial in whatever
efforts they could make in his behalf. Since Paul
mentions a "first defense" which, it seems, succeeded
in clearing him, it is thought that there were at least

two indictments against him. It was the second one that he feared most. Why, it is easy to see, if the first dealt with the causes of the great fire in Rome — with which Paul had absolutely nothing to do, — and the second with the matter of the *religio illicita*, with which he had everything to do. But there may have been more charges, and what they actually were is nowhere stated in a reliable way. — Paul keenly felt the dereliction of his friends, but he nevertheless adds the wish, which amounts to a prayer: **may it not be laid to their account,** μὴ αὐτοῖς λογισθείη, the volitive optative in a wish. The aorist refers to one act and thus points to the final judgment: may it not be imputed to them. This means that Paul forgave them, and that he wished God would do so likewise. Their case then differs materially from that of the coppersmith, where Paul's expectation is certain, because of this man's wicked and persistent obduracy, that the Lord "will render to him according to his works." The sin of the influential Christians who shrank from coming to the apostle's defense was one of weakness, not of obdurate wickedness. In the case of Gentile friends, not yet brought to faith — if there were such in this case, — we may presume that the apostle hoped for their conversion, and that thus this sin of theirs would be forgiven like all the others of their unconverted state. Though the word could apply to them also, if they failed to be converted and were lost, namely that for this forsaking of one of their truest friends in his hour of need, the eternal judge might not lay additional stripes upon them. What a fine thing thus to bear disappointment and wrong in a matter involving one's life and death!

Paul's love bears even this with noble Christian fortitude. Here is an example that cannot be impressed too deeply upon our hearts.

(17) **But the Lord stood by me, and strengthened me; that through me the message might be fully proclaimed, and that all the Gentiles might hear: and I was delivered out of the mouth of the lion.**

Paul, abandoned by the friends who were in a position to help him, was not abandoned by him who is better than any earthly *patronus,* **the Lord** Jesus himself. Παρέστη is intransitive; the 2nd aorist means: "came to my side," *erschien, trat mir zur Seite;* and in this sense: **stood by me.** Παρέστη: *id plus quam παραγίνεσθαι, adesse.* Bengel. Not indeed to influence Paul's judges, but, as the added verb shows, to influence Paul himself and thus his judges: **and strengthened me.** This strengthening had the effect that it made him courageous, able, and strong in his ἀπολογία and in the whole cause which he represented. His success at that first trial he attributes thus wholly to the Lord, who had proved faithful to his humble apostle. Here again the glorified Christ had helped him to fulfil efficiently his calling as an apostle. Conybeare tries to reconstruct the memorable scene: "At one end of the nave was the tribune, in the center of which was placed the magistrate's curule chair of ivory elevated on a platform called the tribunal. Here also sat the council of assessors, who advised the prefect upon the law, though they had no voice in the judgment. On the sides of the tribune were seats for distinguished persons, as well as for parties engaged in the proceedings. Fronting the presiding magistrate stood the prisoner with his accusers and his advocates. The public was admitted into the remainder of the nave and aisles (which was railed off from the portion devoted to the judicial proceedings, and there were also galleries along the whole length of the side aisles — one for men, the other for women. The aisles were roofed over, as was the tribune. The nave was originally left open to the sky. The basilicas were buildings of great size, so that a vast multitude of spectators was always present at any trial which excited public interest. Before such an audience it was that Paul was now called to speak in his defense. His earthly friends had deserted him, but his heavenly Friend stood by him. He was strengthened by the power of Christ's Spirit, and pleaded the cause not of himself only, but of the Gospel. He spoke of Jesus, of his death and his resurrection, so that all the heathen multitude may hear. At the same time he successfully defended himself from the first of the charges brought against him, which perhaps accused him of conspiring with the incendiaries of Rome. He was delivered from the immediate peril, and saved from the ignominious and painful death which might have been his doom had he been convicted on such a charge."

The appended clause with ἵνα has always given trouble to the commentators. Wohlenberg argues at length that Paul meant a preaching and a hearing that was to follow his first acquittal; in fact, that he expected to be acquitted altogether to go on with his preaching, making all the Gentiles to hear. But every statement Paul makes in this letter contradicts this latter opinion: Paul speaks as one who is sure he is about to die; he fully realizes his extreme danger and indulges in no illusions. It is a mistake to think that Paul, who had been in the active work all over the world for about 33 or 34 years still looked forward to an indefinite active period in this work. We have an old man before us, worn with years of labor and trial, not a man in middle life, with most of his work still to do. The κήρυγμα, **message,** or proclamation he means is the Gospel; and πληροφορηθῇ, as in verse 5 means to fulfil, here to complete, or "execute completely" (Stellhorn, and quite a few others). **Might be fully proclaimed** must be read in this sense. But the two verbs in this clause belong together, so we must add as the other side: **and that all the Gentiles might hear.** The aorist ἀκούσωσιν speaks of this hearing as one great and complete fact; a continuous hearing is not meant. Most commentators in reading τὰ πάντα ἔθνη think of Rome as the place where all nations were represented, and that thus they all heard; or they add, like B. Weiss, that the news of Paul's testimony here in Rome would penetrate to all the nations of the Gentiles. Hofmann thinks of a proclamation continued by others, one that would have ceased if Paul had proved recreant in this supreme hour. But there is no reference to others, on the contrary we have the positive δι' ἐμοῦ, with the pronoun in the emphatic form: **by me,** or "through me." Instead of thinking only of what shall yet go out to all the Gentiles, πληροφορηθῇ should lead us to include all Paul's past labors and preaching among the Gentiles, which he was now crowning and thus completing by what he expected to be his final testimony in the great capital of the world. When some years ago he had been tried before the emperor, he had not yet been to the west. But now he had been as far as Spain; he had literally ranged over the whole Roman empire as far as Greek was the world language (he had never tried to reach the "barbarians" by his own personal work). His ministry and κήρυμα, then, he felt would end here, in the center of the great Gentile empire — a glorious fulfilling and completion indeed, when the very rulers of the world themselves now finally heard his "message." In this way it would be indeed an accomplished fact (note the aorist): ἀκούσωσιν πάντα τὰ ἔθνη. The futuristic idea in the subjunctive would include, besides the testimony he had given at his first trial, any other that might be granted him to make in the court sessions yet to come. — **And I was delivered out of the mouth of the lion** is figurative, and reads as if this were not the only report of the apostle's first acquittal which Timothy would receive. The news may have gone out to him before this letter was dispatched, or the bearer of it would himself report all the details to Timothy. There is a reticence here on Paul's part which deserves to be put down to his credit; he does not dilate on his own personal affairs even in so weighty a matter. Let us learn of him. Some have thought of Nero as the lion. If the apostle had meant that he had escaped being cast to the lions in the arena, we should expect him to use the plural, and it is highly improbable that such a penalty would have been inflicted upon a Roman citizen. To escape the lion's mouth is to escape mortal danger. If there is any allusion in the word "lion," it is to Old Testament passages, such as Ps. 22, 22; 7, 2; 35, 17. To refer "lion" here to the devil, as Hofmann, Luther,

Stellhorn, and some others do, and to bring in the thought of spiritual danger, that Paul escaped with his *soul* undamaged, is to go beyond what is actually warranted by the apostle's words. We accordingly refrain from applying 1 Pet. 5, 8 to this word of Paul. Wohlenberg goes too far when he exclaims: "Was this nothing but a victorious preliminary skirmish? That is a simple impossibility." He accordingly thinks Paul was completely acquitted. But, strange to say, the apostle still continued as a prisoner, and no freedom is in sight for him. And in the very next sentence we see whither his thoughts went — to the "heavenly kingdom" of his God. The expression about the lion's mouth is strong, but not too strong for his escape in the first trial, leaving the outcome of the following one at least in doubt.

(18) **The Lord will deliver me from every evil work, and will save me unto his heavenly kingdom: to whom** *be* **the glory forever and ever. Amen.**

Paul takes up the thought of ἐρύσθην, by using the word again, only now in the supreme sense: ῥύσεταί με, the Lord **will deliver** me *etc.* The deliverance he has wrought is a guarantee of the final and complete deliverance he will yet work when now his hour comes. Ὁ κύριος is Jesus, the glorified Redeemer. The preposition ἀπό contrasts with the following εἰς, the one negative, the other positive, the two constituting a whole. **Every evil work** is evil in the moral sense, for πονηρός is not used merely of affliction and tribulation. Nor is this evil something the apostle is himself liable to do, a possible weakening and denial of the faith in his coming trial, but the evil that wicked men plan and execute against him. — The addition: **and will save me unto his heavenly kingdom,** shows how the deliverance is meant — not as a deliverance merely from evil in the course of his earthly life, but a final and complete deliverance by rescue into heaven. The underlying thought is that the evil work of men may succeed and bring the apostle to his death, but by that very death he will be delivered and saved forever. Martyrdom will open paradise for Paul. This is not a sad but a glorious prospect. By the **heavenly kingdom** is meant the counterpart of the earthly kingdom of grace; in the latter we are still subject to the evil works which men may use against us, in that other kingdom all that shall cease. Here is one of the clear passages of Scripture on what shall happen when our souls leave their bodies in death: we shall at once enter the heavenly kingdom, that is heaven, where the heavenly King, Christ, is. There is no intermediate place for the soul, no hades with two compartments, one, paradise, for the righteous, the other, beneath it, an ante-chamber of hell. This perverted notion spoils and darkens the real Christian hope. The body indeed shall sleep in the grave, but the soul shall be where Stephen's soul went at death, where Moses and Elijah are now, in the very presence of God and Christ. The souls of the damned at once go to hell. At the resurrection the body will be raised from the dust, glorified like the soul, joined to it, thereafter to partake of all the bliss of that heavenly kingdom. — Paul's heart is deeply moved as he pens these words. Instead of sad complaint at the thought of a cruel death, his soul is filled with the glow of a golden hope, and utters his joy in the form of praise to God: **to whom** *be* **the glory** — note the article: the glory connected with this whole deliverance and salvation, the glory, excellence, and honor that thus shines forth in his work of grace, mercy, and eternal goodness. It will be an eternal glory: εἰς τοὺς αἰῶνας τῶν αἰώνων, a sonorous and impressive duplication: "unto the ages of the ages." As the result of that saving act will be eternal, so also the credit and honor of him who brings it to pass. — A solemn, impressive ἀμήν is added, like a seal of verity from the fullest assurance of faith. There is here no doubt, no "perhaps," nothing but a certainty which the Lord himself wrought. It is thus that the great apostle faced the end, and it is thus that he finally bowed the head beneath the executioner's sword and went to his eternal reward. As we see the holy light in his eyes, as we look upon his heroic faith, and think then of the wondrous grace of God which changed this man from a blind and wicked Pharisee into an apostle and martyr of this holy Gospel, let us too lift our hearts on high and say with Paul:

**"To the Lord be glory forever and ever.
Amen."**

HOMILETICAL HINTS.

As when the sun, after a long and lovely day, dips to the horizon in the west and glows like a great golden ball, filling the sky with its mighty splendor, so is the soul of the great apostle as he slowly nears the solemn hour of his martyr death. There is no cloud, all is light and glory. It is his faith, refined by years of suffering; it is his hope made fuller and richer as it approached the great hour of its realization. What

Paul preached he lived, and what he preached and lived he finally died. And if his life and labor were grand, a very tower of faith, a great monument of praise to Christ, his death was the fitting capstone of both, a doxology sealed with a pure, golden Amen.

St. Paul too experienced in some measure what came to Christ when at the end he had to stand alone — alone but for God. Let us learn never to depend too much upon men. Not because their comfort is not sweet and their help, as they are able to give it, valuable, but because in the end we are bound, after all, to stand alone, and in that hour there will be but One to stand with us. He is sufficient — now just as well as then. Some would help us, but cannot, others even will not, be their excuse sufficient or not. The Lord lacks neither power nor will, and he makes up for the lack in all others.

Paul was going to his death. Years had passed. I wonder whether in his prison chamber his thoughts went back over those years to the day when he stood by and consented that Stephen should be stoned, and to those dark and ugly days when he harried the church of Christ and brought others to death. Did he remember their faith, their courage, their love, praying for their murderers? Apostle though now he was, all these had left him an example that now he could not but follow. And he followed it indeed. It sounds like an echo of Stephen when he wishes that the friends who had feared to support him might not be charged with their fear and weakness at the last day. And as he felt toward these, so he surely felt also toward his judges and executioners. If not too late, his longing was, that his testimony and his blood might yet win them for Christ.

Paul's concern for his life is secondary, he had something higher entrusted to him — his holy office and ministry. To fulfill that, to complete the great round of the work assigned to him among the Gentiles, this was his chief concern. For this he lived, for this he was ready, when the time would come, to die. What a thought for every minister of to-day! Not that we may have ease, a good living, honor, a fine position, or any other earthly advantage, but that we may do our work, fulfill our calling, omit nothing that is vital to this — whatever else we must lose or forego — such must be our desire. Paul lived for Christ, as his tool and instrument, not for himself; he lived for others, as their servant and intercessor, not for himself. The glory of such a life can be that of every minister of the Gospel in an especially large measure. Let us strive with the Lord's help that this glory may not altogether escape us.

God spares us in most cases — there is no lion's mouth gaping to devour us; no especial danger connected in these quieter times with our profession as Christians and our office as ministers. But there are other ways in which the Lord expects us to stand courageous and undismayed. And if he spares us the fiercer trials of bonds, trial before judges, and bloody martyrdom, we ought the more eagerly show our courage in the confessions he does ask of us, and in the faithfulness our position in an evil and adulterous generation demand. What would become of us if, recreant in these lesser things, the lion after all be allowed to lie in our path?

The features of God's countenance are reflected in a good man. Lisco. — On 'ῥύσεταί με Bengel: *Mala aufert; bona confert.*

The world is full of evil work, full of every kind of such work. And this work is directed against Christ, his kingdom of grace, and all who are in this kingdom. We cannot hope to get through this life without suffering some of the burdens and blows which the evil works in this world aim also at us. But there is one great hope and help for us all: The Lord will at last open the door of his heavenly kingdom and take us in — where the wicked cease from troubling and the weary are at rest. — Our final absolution will come with our dissolution. — We are saved twice: once when we are saved from sin by contrition and faith; and again when we are saved by being ushered from the kingdom of grace into that of glory. And the first salvation is to culminate in the last.

God's glory is the sum of his divine attributes, and this glory inheres in his very essence, because his attributes are identical with his essence. Thus he has, and ever will have, his glory in himself, apart from us and every creature. But God's glory, his blessed attributes have gone forth in the mighty works of his hands. In every one of them we see who he is, they reflect the perfections of his being. Of all these works of his the grandest and most blessed that we are able to know are his works of grace and mercy as they are accomplished in our own hearts and lives. Here the glory of God touches us, and its rays break in on our being, shining with a thousand glorious flashes. Here is all his love, his wisdom and might, his patience and longsuffering, his goodness and kindness, his justice and holiness. Shall we refuse to respond to this glory? Shall it recede from us with its beneficent rays, to strike us down with its vindictive and punitive fire? God's glory and perfection cannot cease, he cannot change or deny himself. But we can fall crushed beneath his glory, if we do not fall down and worship it, and give our hearts and tongues to sing its praise as it blesses us. — To live with Christ in the kingdom of his glory is eternal glory for us.

The Amen that has God's truth behind it is an echo of that truth, though weak human lips utter it. The amens that many speak so lightly, when they have put behind this form of assurance nothing but their own foolish reasonings and imaginations, are only an echo of their own hollowness and falseness. Only God's promises are yea and amen; they alone have behind them the Lord's "Verily, verily, I say unto you." Let us plant our hearts on his Word, then sing his praise in joyful songs, and close with Amen.

St. Paul's Death Preparation.

I. *Serene trust in the Lord's help.*
II. *Forgiving love toward his erring friends.*
III. *Ardent faithfulness for his final task.*
IV. *Joyful hope of eternal deliverance.*

The Lord at Paul's Side to the Last.

I. *To aid him in his last trials.*
II. *To help him finish and crown his work.*
III. *To lift him into eternal glory.*

2 Tim. 4, 16-18. 247

When the Last Hour Draws Nigh.

I. *Think of the Lord.*
   1) All his past help. 2) All his present support.
II. *Think of the Gospel.*
   1) What it means to you. 2) What its message means to others likewise.
III. *Think of the heavenly kingdom.*
   1) Your entrance. 2) Its blessedness. 3) God's glory for ever and ever.

The Lord's Eternal Deliverance.

For St. Paul it was:
I. *The crown of the Gospel message he preached.*
II. *The strength of his soul during the trials of life.*
III. *The hope he realized in the hour of death.*

St. Paul's Doxology in the Face of Death.

I. *God's grace had filled his life.*
II. *God's grace would shine in his death.*

St. Paul's Final Soli Deo Gloria.

It summed up:
I. *The Gospel of grace he had preached.*
II. *The life of faith and love he had lived.*
III. *The blessedness and joy he would enter upon.*

Soli Deo Gloria.